W9-ARV-710

Praise for *I'll Miss You Too*

Like sitting down for a chat with a neighbor who has been through the process, *I'll Miss You Too* offers a candid and friendly story of one particular family's experiences. And the authors' consistently upbeat message, that they made it through the process and emerged closer than ever, will be reassuring for anyone facing a similar struggle. Their message of openness and mutual respect is one that many anxious parents and students could benefit from hearing.

—Excerpt from NACAC book review, *The Journal of College Admission Counseling*, Leslie Goddard, assistant director of admission and financial aid at Northwestern University, Illinois

This is a unique and fresh approach to dealing with very real college anxieties and family communication issues. The differing perspectives of student and parent are eye-opening and informative. A great book for families to read together throughout the college years.

—Thomas McManus, director of college counseling, Tatnall School

A great resource to use throughout the entire college journey—from acceptance to graduation.

—Suzanne Ketcham, former assistant director of admission, University of Miami

Once started, it was hard to put down! We have taken the journey through the "doors" twice with our two sons and now are taking it with our daughter. *I'll Miss You Too* hits home! It is an excellent guide and we truly wish we had read it when our firstborn was entering his senior year in high school. We recommend it to all parents and students who are getting ready for their own journey.

—Donna and Clark Collins, parents

I'll Miss You Too provides practical advice to parents and children on how to understand each other during one of the toughest transition periods of our interdependent lives. With two sons and two daughters between the ages of nine and fifteen, it has, thankfully, opened my eyes for the journey ahead. It will be a good preparation for our family as the children take their first steps away from home. The authors reached both our hearts and heads with their insightful dialogue!

—Fred Honold, parent

I'll Miss You Too was like a trip down memory lane. It touched so many chords in me as I remembered the emotional times. This book also opened my eyes as to what my parents must have been experiencing. For students, it is a must!

—Stephanie Tipton, graduate of the University of Miami

I cannot find a book that addresses significant and germane transitional issues as adeptly, cogently, honestly, and sincerely as this.

—Jim Bixby, dean of student services, Lincoln College, Illinois

I just loved this book! It helped me realize my mother's perspective during this transition—so much so that I called her as soon as I was finished reading it! I recommend it to any incoming freshman.

—Marianne S. Mitchell, student, Syracuse University

As both parent and educator, I highly recommend this book. It provides helpful tips on how to cope with the inevitable emotional ups and downs [of sending a child to college]. I am grateful to the authors for taking their experiences to heart and sharing them with others.

—Susan Thurman, PhD, associate editor and scholarship chair,
The National Society of High School Scholars

An eye-opening book about the issues and surprises that parents and their kids ought to talk about before and after getting into college. It's personal and practical—especially because it gives insights and observations from both sides, the parents' and the child's.

—Rev. Andrew Costello, educator and author,
Annapolis, Maryland

This book is unique! Poignant and fun, it opens positive discussion and planning between students and parents. It is a great resource designed for the emotional transition to college.

—Jeff Stahlman, director of college counseling,
New Albany High School, Columbus, Ohio

As a guidance counselor and a parent, I can't imagine my practice or my home without this book. There is an honesty in it that should lead to important family discussions before a child goes away to college.

—Steve Peifer, director of college guidance,
Rift Valley Academy, Kijabe, Kenya

We were having great anxiety when Sara was ready to go off to Yale and wondering whether we really understood what she was thinking and going through. This book is dead-on correct with its insights, anecdotes, and advice. My wife and I recommend it to other parents as a must read in preparation for the college experience.

—Mark A. Aronchick, Esq., parent,
Cherry Hill, New Jersey

I recommend buying two: one for you and one for your child! The book has valuable advice on every subject imaginable, even ones that you may not feel comfortable discussing.

—Shannon Sheridan, recent college graduate,
New York, New York

I'll Miss You Too

Margo E. Bane Woodacre, MSW & Steffany Bane

I'll
Miss You
Too

What Will Change, What Will Not
and How We'll Stay Connected

Margo E. Bane Woodacre, MSW & Steffany Bane

SOURCEBOOKS, INC.®
NAPERVILLE, ILLINOIS

Copyright © 2006 by Margo E. Bane Woodacre and Steffany Bane
Cover and internal design © 2006 by Sourcebooks, Inc.
Cover photo: Getty Images
Author photo by Dick duBroff, Final Focus
Sourcebooks and the colophon are registered trademarks of Sourcebooks, Inc.

All rights reserved. No part of this book may be reproduced in any form or by any electronic or
mechanical means including information storage and retrieval systems—except in the case of brief
quotations embodied in critical articles or reviews—without permission in writing from its publisher,
Sourcebooks, Inc.

This publication is designed to provide accurate and authoritative information in regard to the subject matter covered. It is sold with the understanding that the publisher is not engaged in rendering
legal, accounting, or other professional service. If legal advice or other expert assistance is required,
the services of a competent professional person should be sought.—*From a Declaration of Principles Jointly
Adopted by a Committee of the American Bar Association and a Committee of Publishers and Associations*

This book is not intended as a substitute for medical advice from a qualified physician. The intent of
this book is to provide accurate general information in regard to the subject matter covered. If medical advice or other expert help is needed, the services of an appropriate medical professional should
be sought.

All brand names and product names used in this book are trademarks, registered trademarks, or trade
names of their respective holders. Sourcebooks, Inc., is not associated with any product or vendor in
this book.

Published by Sourcebooks, Inc.
P.O. Box 4410, Naperville, Illinois   60567-4410
(630) 961-3900
Fax: (630) 961-2168
www.sourcebooks.com

Originally published in 2001 by American Literary Press, Inc.

Library of Congress Cataloging-in-Publication Data

Woodacre, Margo E. Bane.
  I'll miss you too : what will change, what will not and how we'll stay connected / Margo E. Bane
Woodacre.
    p. cm.
  ISBN-13: 978-1-4022-0641-2
  ISBN-10: 1-4022-0641-0
  1. College student orientation—United States. 2. College students—Family relationships—
United States. I. Bane, Steffany. II. Title.

LB2343.32.W66 2005
378.1'98—dc22

                              2005025018

Printed and bound in the United States of America.
VP 10 9 8 7 6 5 4 3

To Mom (Mom-mom) and Angie,

with love

Contents

Acknowledgments

The greatest pleasure in writing our book has come from the opportunity to travel and learn from the many people we encountered, people of various ages, races, and economic status. Along with our family and friends at home, these people helped make our new edition a reality. For their support and encouragement, we are truly grateful.

Special thanks go to Bill Bane for his belief and support in this project from the very beginning; Ernie Woodacre for his insight, patience, and creative editing; Valerie Woodruff for her research and editing skills, promotional ideas, and friendship; the many guidance and college counselors, students, and parents who were willing to share their feelings and personal stories; and our editor, Carrie Obry, and the Sourcebooks team for their expertise and enthusiasm in the creation of the new edition.

We are also thankful for long mother-daughter walks and talks, faith, and the yellow door on Andover Road.

Preface

The creation of this book, originally published as *Doors Open from Both Sides,* resulted from a decision that we, as mother and daughter, made while dealing with our own emotional challenges during the off-to-college transition. As we wrote the book, we learned more about each other and how differently we handled many issues. The more we learned and understood, the more open and effective our communication became.

The 2001 publishing of our book and subsequent speaking engagements about the college transition provided the opportunity for us to speak to parents, students, and school counselors from all parts of the country. During our visits, people were eager to learn from our journey as well as share their own stories and experiences about this significant life transition.

A new book has evolved from this knowledge. The collective wisdom gained has enriched its content. We hope that *I'll Miss You Too,* through its frank and sometimes poignant messages, will help you, as parents and students, share a healthy college transition. Know that whatever it is you are experiencing, you are not alone.

— Margo and Steffany

Introduction

When one door closes, another opens, but we often look so long and so regretfully upon the closed door that we do not see the one that has opened for us.

—Alexander Graham Bell

For most of us, going through life's transitions is like opening new doors. As we open them, we discover surprises, new findings, new challenges, and new fears. Sometimes, we need to close the doors to put closure on matters. Sometimes, we need to work to keep them open.

One major life transition occurs at the stage when the young adult leaves home to go off to college. This transition brings new experiences and challenges for both the parent and the child. Despite having lived under the same roof for a number of years, parents and children inevitably have different perspectives on some aspects of life. Consequently, experiencing the college separation process can affect them in different ways. This book, written by a mother and her daughter, describes how we each saw, felt, and learned from this particular transition. Our two points of view represent both sides of the transition—both sides of the door.

With the transition come phases that have their own joys, their own challenges, and their own fears. The book starts with the senior year of high school and carries the reader through to the senior year in college, focusing a chapter on each of the transitional phases ("doors") along the way. Drawing on our own personal journey, as well as experiences shared by other families and counselors, we provide poignant and humorous stories with helpful advice on how to avoid some of the common traps parents and students can fall into during each phase of the transition. This book is most helpful to families when read by both parent and student.

I'll Miss You Too presents specific insight into what parent and child experience during what family therapists Carter and McGoldrick (1989) call the "launching children and moving on" stage of life. For the young adult leaving the nest, this stage can be a time of excitement, but also confusion and fear. It is also the time for him or her to start to differentiate from the emotional program of the family, formulate personal life goals, and become an independent self.

For parents of the college-bound child, the process of letting go is not new. In a broad sense, parents start to experience the separation process through events such as their child's stages of toddlerhood, first days of school, and first vacation away from home and family. Despite these early experiences, the sense of loss and separation anxiety can be more pronounced when the young adult child goes off on his or her own—whether to attend college, to take a job away from home, to get married, or to join the service. For the parents left in the empty nest, it is the time to learn to let go, redefine personal identity and relationships, and look ahead to the future as they start to change the relationship with their maturing child.

When young ones leave home, parents realize that they have more personal freedom, but of course, so do their children. From here on, parents will always have less control over the departing child. The maturing young adult feels a growing and sometimes exhilarating sense of freedom. Yet, while perhaps not always recognizing it, they still have an ongoing need for continued support and guidance. The needs and views of the two generations and the temperamental relationship of parent and child can often become challenging. Fortunately, with a mutual commitment to understanding each other, this time of life, despite its stresses, can be rewarding and fulfilling. As Erma Bombeck once wrote in her column:

Wouldn't it be wonderful if parents could look at their teenagers and say, "I want you to stay, but you can't." Wouldn't it be wonderful if teenagers could look at their parents and say, "I don't want to leave, but I must." It's so much better to close the door gently on childhood than to slam it.

For young adults raised with the security of a home and family for seventeen to twenty years, the transition into independence and freedom is a new experience. For parents who devoted the same amount of time to guiding and supporting their children, this change can create a large, empty hole in their everyday lives. There are no formal guidelines for managing emotions during this important transition. Hopefully, what we've learned from writing this book can help readers learn how to "close the door gently on childhood."

I'll Miss You Too was written with love, sweat, and tears. Together, as mother and daughter, we recalled our personal challenges and assessed how they opened our eyes to our differences and our similarities. We drew from the personal journals we kept over several years and exchanged ideas through telephone contact, emails, and visits. Through this communication, we discovered that while we were both going through the same transition, we faced different types of challenges in dealing with it. Most importantly, we realized that often we made assumptions about what the other was feeling. We eventually learned that many of these assumptions had been wrong. Together, we decided to write a book that could be helpful to others facing the same kind of challenges.

Emotional Beginnings

Thoughts from Mom

September (Journal entry)

My forty-seven years of life have brought challenges, but none has touched my emotions more than the approaching empty nest syndrome. This stage has been filled with a mixture of joy, excitement, fear, and loneliness. I have become more introspective and questioning about who I am and who I am becoming. Suddenly, I am looking for more meaning to my life. Is this middle age or true growth?

As the mother of an only child (and a single mother for many years), I worked outside the home but considered motherhood my main job and my joy. To me, the empty nest syndrome was simply a term to describe the phase of life when parents learn to adjust after their children move out. It sounded so simple! For some parents, it meant the freedom of having their personal lives back. Despite this, I rarely found a parent who didn't feel a sense of uneasiness when approaching this new phase. Whether the parent faces the departure of an only child, a first child, or a last child, the realization begins to set in that life is about to take on a new dimension.

Thoughts from Steff

Leaving home for the first time can be a scary experience. For me, it was both scary and exciting. During most of my senior year of high school, I thought I was ready to go. When I got accepted into my first-choice college, I knew it was the time to go! Doubts soon set in, however, when I thought of all the things I was leaving behind: my familiar day-to-day schedule, special people, personal possessions, and the safety of my bedroom. Most of all, I was leaving my secure life at home. Although these mixed emotions were confusing and bothersome to me, I sensed that the time was right to move on and become more independent.

In high school we talked a lot about "getting out" in the same way prisoners would talk about escaping from jail. We were ready to go off to college, start a job, meet new people, move out of the house, and be on our own. When the time actually arrived, however, fears surfaced from out of nowhere!

My choice was to go relatively far away to college. I wanted a college that specialized in my academic interests, but I also wanted to have my freedom. I wanted to prove to others that I could make it on my own. Yes, there were fears and doubts, but I felt it had to be done. I think that Mom wanted to have me closer to home, but she didn't want to stand in my way. At that time, it was important for me to know that I had loving family and friends that supported my decision to move so far from home. With this support, I decided to follow my instincts and my heart. As I look back, I am truly glad I did it.

A Time for Every Season in Life

by Margo

Fall is my favorite season. It has always been a season for special events and challenges in my life. From each of these, I felt a sense of personal growth. I was born in the fall, I left home in the fall, I was married in the fall, I had my baby in the fall, I was divorced in the fall, and my father passed away in the fall. This fall, my daughter will leave home to venture into adulthood.

I believe that, like the seasons of nature, we experience seasons in our lives. As fall arrives this year, the change in color and the loss of leaves represents something more to me. As each leaf falls, it makes me more aware of the beauty and the passing of a very special season of my life—that of raising my child. This stage of motherhood (this "season") has been a special one, filled with colorful events, learning, and growth. This has been the best time of my life. And just as my favorite season fades and the vibrant leaves fall from the trees, I see this vibrant time of my life fading. I realize that Steffany will soon be leaving home and moving into her adult years, and that I will be losing my role as it has been, as Mom.

I know that winter approaches. And, like the bare and silent season of winter, life at home will seem to take a rest. The house will be quiet, my schedule less busy, and my life, as it has been, will be changed. There is a knowing, a faith, that this part of my life will go on, just at a different pace and in a different space in time—just as it should.

At the same time, my excitement soars with what is ahead. Spring brings a newness, freshness, and exhilaration by returning the appearance of life to nature, with lush fullness and color. And I trust that this new phase of my life will bring the same energy and beauty, a new fullness to my everyday life and richness to my relationship with my daughter, as an adult.

I do believe that the seasons change to remind us of our ever-changing lives. Exhilaration, rest, and growth. Always constant, all as it should be. And beyond this space and time, there is the reminder to enjoy the moment. After all, that is all we really have.

FOR BETTER OR FOR WORSE ©2005 Lynn Johnston Productions. Dist. By Universal Press Syndicate. Reprinted with permission. All rights reserved.

Chapter 1

The High School Senior Year
The Revolving Door

Entering the senior year of high school is like moving through a revolving door: attention needs to be focused on making a good exit! The senior year calls for careful planning for that exit, whether it be to college or to a job. Either way, it is a year full of activities that focus on the child's future. If the goal is college, much of the school year revolves around choosing and getting into a college.

It is also a year for those parents facing an imminent empty nest to reflect upon the past and think about their future. Just as high school seniors remind themselves, "this is the last game, the last test, the last dance, the last play," the parents begin to realize that they, too, will be involved in a series of "lasts." Questions suddenly enter their minds: "What's next?" "What will be my future role as a parent?" "How can I handle this?"

Mom

The term "empty nest" really hit home for me during my daughter's high school senior year:

September (Journal entry)

Today is the first day of Steffany's senior year in high school. Hard to believe, but true. I woke up early thinking about it. I recalled taking her to her first day of kindergarten and shortly thereafter watching her walk independently into the first grade. On both of those occasions, I went home, cried, and asked myself, Where has the time gone?

Now, years later, I feel like crying again. The next first for Steff will be a move toward being out on her own. As a mother, I am aware that an important part of my own life is in major transition, and this change is somewhat frightening. I feel a sense of excitement mixed with a degree of apprehension.

Steff has started her college essays and applications and feels she has a good chance of getting into some of her chosen colleges. I am enjoying helping her with these important decisions. It's a busy time in her life and I believe she is ready for the change. I only hope I am!

The first college night at the high school was overwhelming to us when we learned about all the decisions we'd soon have to make about final SAT schedules, applications, essays, and college interviews. It brought back memories of my own high school senior year. I remembered how taking the SATs was nerve-racking, but it started to become clear to me that the pressures on today's student to get into college are much heavier than in my years. The demand for robust SAT scores certainly seemed more of a factor now than it did twenty years ago. Another new factor was the abundance of choice! If my memory had it right, my friends and I applied to maybe two or three colleges, which, in most cases, were local. The college counselor, on this evening, recommended applying to many schools.

I glanced around the band room to see if the other parents appeared as surprised and overwhelmed as I was. I felt somewhat relieved as I heard some of their questions and concerns. I was not alone. We all seemed to want our children to follow the right course and, given their interests and capabilities, get into the best school for them.

> Some kids take charge of their own hunt for college, others work together with their parents, and some let their parents do it for them.
>
> —College counselor, Maryland

As a congenital worrier, I left the meeting feeling a need to get started on what seemed a large list of college-related chores. I became torn between my good intention to hand over responsibility to Steffany and my worry-based, impatient need to jump in and help her get them done.

Fortunately, Steffany was somewhat diligent (with some coaxing) about meeting her responsibilities and deadlines. Others helped with this seemingly large task. Steff's high school counselor was very important in keeping her on her toes with the deadlines. Her dad helped her with applications and took her on some of the college visits. My husband, her stepfather, supported Steffany by helping proofread her essays.

I felt it important to support my daughter's choice of schools. As matters developed, I was surprised but pleased to see that she seemed to have definite opinions about where she wanted to go and what she wanted to study. In contrast, I remembered making my personal choice of colleges according to my then-boyfriend's choice. My choice turned out to be the right school for me, but I was proud that Steff seemed to be making her decisions for herself. I felt that this truly was a healthy sign of independence.

I must admit that the location of the school that she chose bothered me because I held hopes that she would not be far away. My view was that a reasonable car ride from home was okay, but an airplane ride seemed too far. Although I struggled silently with this, I did not mention it to Steff and continued to show my support for her choice.

According to comments from many college counselors, some parents often want to make the college decision *for* their child. Unfortunately, some parents favor schools connected with prestige or family tradition. Parents need to be careful in this regard. Obviously, their input is important, but it should be based primarily on consideration for the student's aspirations. When undue pressure is put on the child to get into their parents' or grandparents' alma mater, the child can feel forced and unhappy. As one counselor from a Maryland private school advised:

The choice should not be what college sticker a parent wants on the car, but what college is a good fit for the child.

With the costs of tuition climbing so high, the family financial situation is becoming a bigger issue in the selection of a college. Often, the child's choice does not fit the financial capabilities of the family. With financial aid widely available, however, it is likely that financial matters can be worked out. Also, keep in mind the price tag given to you by the school does not take the student's financial aid package into account. In the end, it's possible that the expensive school will end up costing less than the school with the cheaper price tag. For whatever reasons a college is chosen, it is imperative that the child feel good about it.

Once Steffany's applications were sent in, we began the anxious wait for responses. For some of her friends, acceptances arrived early. The word would come: "So-and-so got accepted." These announcements placed more pressure on us.

Steffany had applied for early acceptance; she knew with certainty which college she wanted and had applied to second choices only at the suggestion of her counselor. This approach had its benefits, but it also had its risks. In Steffany's mind, there was only one college for her, and if she were accepted there, her enthusiasm for college would be sky-high. My unspoken fear was that her first-choice college might not select her.

> My biggest fear is that my parents will choose my college for me and it won't be my choice!
>
> —High school senior, Pennsylvania

We waited for the mail like we were waiting for a lucky lotto number. We had been told that acceptances would be in bulkier envelopes. One day, a thin envelope arrived from her chosen college. I was traveling and intuitively called home. On the other end was a tearful, depressed daughter who felt that her world had ended. Steffany had been deferred. At that moment, she could not distinguish between *deferred* and *rejected*. She clearly needed a shoulder to cry on. A thousand miles from home, how helpless I felt!

The universe smiled on Steffany, however, when, during the following month, our mail included a bulky envelope from college choice Number One. I remember pulling it from the mailbox and feeling my heart race. I nervously held it up to the light and attempted to read through the envelope. I did see the word "Congratulations!" and as a parent, I felt relieved and ecstatic. We had hit our lottery!

Throughout the senior year, it had been helpful to share feelings with other parents. At sporting and school events, we found ourselves talking about joys, fears, and the growing sense of sadness about the approaching transition. It was helpful for me to know that I was not alone with my feelings. I remember one mother telling me:

Each time I drive down the driveway at school, I am aware that I won't be doing this next year and I have a sick feeling in the pit of my stomach. I already have planned an alternate driving route for the next year so I won't have to go by the school!

I also remember prom night when parents gathered at each other's homes to take the last high school dance photos. As our well-coiffed, elegant, and handsomely dressed young people smiled for the cameras, we shook our heads in disbelief that this was yet another school *last*. We reminisced about the memories of our children's first dance at middle school and once again asked each other where the time had gone.

Senior year was filled with many emotions and culminated with graduation. For many parents and their children, graduation was an emotional experience. For months, we were wrapped up in the excitement leading up to the actual event. Suddenly, there we were, sitting at the final high school event. One teary-eyed father of an only child whispered to me as we watched our children receive their diplomas:

> It's unfortunate that so many parents focus on getting the kids into the "right" college instead of guiding them and letting them make the decisions.
> —College counselor, Ohio

It seems like I have been sitting in this gym for five years cheering on Jim's teams. I'm excited for him, but I know I've become very attached to this era and it saddens me that it's over.

For that parent and the rest of us, an era was over. We were now aware that the college era would provide its own mixture of feelings and, no doubt, challenges.

Steff

Finally, I'm a senior, and among the oldest kids in the school! Even before I was a teenager, I dreamed of being a senior and ruling the school. When senior year arrived, I was ready for it. This meant senior privileges, my own parking spot, more free time and, not to forget, college was right around the corner. We all threw around the word "college" like it was no big deal, and we felt extremely cool saying it.

I found my long-term friends increasingly important to me as we went along with the flow of our last school year. We had had so many good times and we cherished them. Now we sensed that our closeness could be ending.

College was becoming more of a reality than a fantasy because of the forms, essays, and everything that had to be done for applications. Although I had visited my favorite college choices, my mother and I were still making weekend trips to nearby colleges. During this period, my schedule was jam-packed with priorities involving schoolwork, sports, and applications. I felt I had never been faced with so many deadlines in my life.

I never realized how much preparation was needed to even apply to college. Standardized testing—my nemesis. I had never been a fan of bubble testing or any kind of computer that graded me. SAT prep courses were taken at school and a bunch of my friends took classes after school as well. I'd see them carrying around these huge workbooks and reading materials. The whole idea freaked me out because 1.) I had never excelled at timed, standardized tests and 2.) it was hard to imagine that a college could accept or deny me based on a random number.

I felt I was more a personality than a test score! I would much rather be interviewed by an admissions department. At the same time, I realized it might be a bit tiring for them to interview a twenty-five-thousand-student applicant pool. I couldn't bear the thought of going through it again. I did find out my first-choice school was coming to do interviews in my area, and I rushed to get my face seen and known. Some people work best behind a pencil and others work best face to face.

The whole idea of going off to college was exciting: new places, new faces, choice of major, and a class schedule that I could select on my own—so much freedom! My friends and I would meet during our breaks at school and chat about how we were ready to graduate. By midyear, our familiar, robot-like schedules were becoming a bit boring, but we still felt comfortable and safe.

Over the past twelve years, I had grown up with the same people at the same school. While we always separated and did our own things in the summer, we would return in the fall to the same friends with new stories and experiences to share. It was exciting to hear what travels and stories accumulated over these long three months. After doing this for twelve years and knowing next year there was no school schedule to bring us back together, I started to sense that the life I was used to was about to change.

Students can react in different ways to their last year in high school. Some feel few emotional ties to their schools and are ecstatic at the prospect of leaving. However, along with most of my friends, I was starting to feel a bit melancholy about the approaching end.

I think I felt this first through my involvement in sports. While suiting up for my last basketball game, I realized that I would never again put on my high school jersey for a game. There were five seniors on our team, and we were all close. After our last game, there was complete silence on our bus ride home. This was when I lost it. My sports career as a senior was now over. My senior teammates felt it, too. The final basketball game was a catalyst for what became a downward spiral of worries. There were so many "what ifs" clouding my head: What if I don't find happiness out there? What if I don't get the opportunity to play team sports again? What if my friends move on and forget me? This was the first time I truly realized how important this passing phase of my life had been to me. I began to think about all my lasts—my last game, my last prom, my last performance, my last test, my last class—all the way up to my last day as a senior.

I also made myself focus on what was ahead. There was something both scary and soothing about the unknown. Although I must admit, constantly hanging over me was the fear of not getting accepted into my first choice or even any of my college choices. Each day my heart pounded as I checked the mail. Knowing how eager Mom could be, I had asked her not to open any responses from colleges. One day, I returned home to find a thin envelope embossed with my favorite college logo. Aware of the bad reputation of small envelopes, I tore into it with shaking hands and read:

It is very difficult to get in through early application and your application will be placed in blah blah blah...

I only focused on the opening words; the rest of the letter was a blur. I had completely zoned out because I was now an official basket case! I was devastated. Mom was away on business and not around to console me. She was the one I needed the most.

Hearing Mom's voice on the phone that night, I got emotional and sobbed like a baby. To me, my fear of not getting accepted had become a reality. Despite my parents assuring me that my chances were still good, I was deeply disappointed, somewhat embarrassed, and fell into a slump for the next week. I did not mention the letter to my friends.

As things turned out, I hadn't been rejected. That "blah blah blah" had actually read, "...you will be placed in regular admission." Within the next few weeks, I arrived home to find a thicker envelope from my favorite college. I opened the letter to find a congratulatory letter of acceptance. Mom put a baseball cap with the college logo on my head (somehow she knew what was in the letter) and I felt on top of the world. I had no idea of the emotional journey that lay ahead.

After our celebration, my efforts turned to getting ready for the next phase. Now I couldn't wait to head off to college. With my biggest fear removed, the road ahead seemed clear and I felt ready for the challenge.

Here's a sample of our survey of parents and high school seniors. We separately asked parents and their son or daughter the following questions.

Survey 1

Question: *How prepared do you feel your child is to go off on his own?*

Dad: Lord knows, I've tried! Honestly, I don't think he will make it. At home, he can't even get himself up for school in the morning.

Question: *How well prepared do you feel to be on your own?*

Son: I'm ready! The only fear is that my dad will be on my case all the time.

Survey 2

Question: *How prepared do you feel your child is to go off on her own?*

Mom: She is ready. She's happy and confident and very mature for her age. She will probably be everyone else's "mom" on campus!

Question: *How well prepared do you feel to be on your own?*

Daughter: Not sure if I'm ready. I've worked at the beach for a summer on my own but going as far away as I am to school, I am beginning to feel scared.

Trap Doors

Tips from Mom for Parents

✳ **Validate your feelings:** Accept and respect your feelings during this stage of your life. Facing change is one of the biggest human fears. The "Launching of Children" phase is a major life transition and feelings of apprehension on the part of all family members are normal. Be thankful to know that these feelings represent a positive attachment between parents and child.

✳ **Talk about your emotions:** Share your experience with and get support from your partner, your family, or a friend who has been through or is going through this kind of a transition. You will not feel so alone with your feelings, and you might be able to help each other get through this experience.

✳ **Keep a personal journal:** A journal can help you express your thoughts and emotions in a very personal and non-threatening form. It will help to acknowledge and validate your feelings. Down the road, it will provide memories of an important period in the life of your child and yourself.

* **Don't be surprised if your student's behavior seems distant at this point:** College counselors remind parents that it is not unusual for their children to start acting out at this stage of the game. This technique is often used to distance themselves from their parents before they leave for college.

* **Stay organized:** The high school senior year is busy with activities and important deadlines. Keeping a calendar of events and lists of things to do and due dates helps everybody move effectively through a hectic schedule.

* **Enjoy the moment:** There will be exciting and memorable moments during your child's senior year. Make the most of them. Try not to get overwhelmed by the "to do" lists, and take one day at a time.

* **Get help from the college counselor at the high school:** It is important for both the parents and students to get acquainted with the counselor. College counselors know the ropes with the college application system, and they can be helpful guides along the way.

* **Do not be surprised if your student has no idea of what he wants to study in college at this point:** Be patient with your child on choice of school and studies. According to college counselors across the country, less than 10 percent of the senior classes have a good sense of direction when it comes to selecting their area of study.

✳ **Start allowing opportunities for your child to practice increasing independence:** Let's face it; your student will be without you at college. Hopefully, at this point, you have provided the opportunities for her to make decisions and take responsibilities throughout the high school years. During the summer before college, allow more independence when appropriate. This is the time to help your student practice functioning without the safety net of Mom and Dad. They need to develop a sense of responsible independence.

Tips from Steff for Students

✳ **Visit the campuses of the colleges being considered:** Certainly try to visit and tour the campuses of your primary choices. It is important to get a feel for the environment. If you know someone who is already attending one of your favorite colleges, arrange for a weekend visit. This way, you will capture the true flavor of campus life and have a chance to ask the current students important questions.

✳ **Don't be hard on yourself if you don't know your area of studies yet:** You don't need to declare any major at this point. Odds are that it is too early for you to make this choice. Take time, though, to research your areas of interests. This may help guide you in selecting an area of study. Beware, though, that your interests might change during your years at college!

* **Know the difference between "deferred" and "rejected":** Understand that being deferred is not being rejected. Deferrals simply put you on the next list to be considered. (How calmly I can say that now!)

* **Don't give up on your goal:** If you receive a deferral or a rejection to your favorite college, don't give up. Write or call the college admissions person or department and, without being critical or defensive, share your disappointment as well as your continuing determination to get in. Colleges want students who really want to be there.

* **Be aware that your parents might get on your nerves:** Seniors are so busy with finishing up high school and college applications. Don't be surprised if your parents get on your nerves with constant reminders about things that need to be done. In my case, although Mom was a bit of a pain, she did keep me from procrastinating on important matters.

* **Don't wish your time away!** During your senior year, spend as much time as you can doing things you love to do and spend it with the people you want to be with! The last year of high school moves too quickly. Try to enjoy each moment.

From surveys of parents and students across the country, these were selected as the ten biggest fears about the off-to-college transition:

Ten Biggest Off-to-College Fears for Parents

✻ Overall safety for my child

✻ Losing communication with my child

✻ Developing a new relationship with my child

✻ My child making poor judgments

✻ The dangers of drugs and alcohol

✻ My child's inability to handle newfound freedom

✻ My inability to let go

✻ Dealing with the new Empty Nest at home

✻ My changed role as parent

✻ My changed relationship with my spouse at home and the effects on the rest of my family

Ten Biggest Off-to-College Fears for Students

✻ Not being happy at the school I choose

✻ Disliking my roommate

✻ That my parents won't trust me on my own

✻ Missing my high school friends

✻ Homesickness

✻ That college won't be what I expect

✻ Choosing a major

✻ That I will not meet the school's academic standards

✻ Constant contact from my parents

✻ Financial problems

Chapter 2

The Summer before College
The Busy Door

The summer before freshman year is unusually busy, filled with shopping, packing, and preparing for the move to college. Mail will arrive frequently from the colleges with information, course selections, applications for dorms, and schedules for fall classes. This summer is like a whirlwind of activity culminating in an emotional send-off.

Mom

During these months, I found that my earlier feelings of apprehension had diminished. The course ahead was set. My daughter was getting ready for an important step in her life, and we were working together to get ready for it. At the same time, I knew that for her, every moment that she spent with family and friends was precious. The friends going on to college shared their own news about potential roommates, school schedules, and general excitement about the new stage in their lives.

Most of my focus was on the necessary shopping, paperwork, and packing. I followed the lists sent to us from the college, shopped the local back-to-school sales, and compared notes with other parents, hoping not to miss anything important with the off-to-college preparation. I tried to include my daughter as much as possible, but she was too busy with her part-time job and social life. I didn't like the fact that *I* was the only one doing the preparation.

By the middle of August, I felt I had accomplished my part in what needed to be done toward Steffany's departure. Suddenly, activity seemed to cease in my role as "transition manager." I became increasingly conscious of the fact that my child was soon to leave home and venture out into the adult world. It was then that my emotions began to intensify:

August (Journal entry)

Here I sit, looking at clean and pressed clothes folded ready for Steff to pack for college. Her trunk is already filled and closed. Just two days left before the move to Florida. I hear that it is harder before our children leave than it is when they are actually away. I don't know about that. I do know how quiet and lonely this house will be. Oh dear, I'll miss her. I ask myself at this point, How did my mom deal with my leaving for college so well? I don't remember seeing her anxious or sad and we were close, too. Why is it so hard for me?

When not focusing on the physical responsibilities of getting Steffany ready for college, I found my happiness about her new adventure sometimes giving way to doubts. My biggest worry was about her safety while being on her own. For the most part, Steff had displayed much responsibility over her teen years. There had been occasional issues with her grades not always being what they could be, the intermittent party at someone's home where there was alcohol and rowdiness, and the time she had been caught drinking beer in a parking lot, but we had been blessed up to this point with no serious emergency situations. Most importantly, our communication seemed to remain open and, if needed, she was disciplined appropriately for breaking our house rules.

Now Steff was heading off to a life of total freedom. I realized that I had no control over the hours she kept, her study habits, her partying, or the friends with whom she chose to spend her time. Would she act responsibly and wisely? Had I done a good job of teaching her right from wrong?

I found it more difficult to openly communicate my concerns with her during the busy summer months. She had distanced herself from me more than usual, and when I attempted to have necessary talks about this, she accused me of having little trust in her. It seemed that our usually good communication was waning.

The Time Finally Arrives

Southern colleges tend to start earlier. For that reason, Steff was one of the first of her friends to leave. The night before she left for college was so busy! The phone rang nonstop and many of her high school friends came to say goodbye and wish her well. There was laughter and there were tears. Her boyfriend and closest friends stayed until late, waiting as long as they possibly could before having to say goodbye. I felt it important to give them their privacy. Exhausted from the preparation and surge of activity, I went to bed early knowing the morning would come all too soon. It did.

First to get up, I found the house quiet. There wasn't much to do. The car was packed. Preparation was over and the move was upon us. I had a long drive ahead. My feelings of fear and sadness began to emerge again:

August (Journal entry)

I woke up early this morning with a gnawing in my stomach. Today is the day that I have thought about over this entire year. Steff leaves for college, for real. Life here at home will be so different. I'm already feeling a sense of loss. I have felt this feeling before; it is similar to the feeling I had when my father passed away. Is this normal to feel this way? I don't like the feeling.

On Our Way

The goodbyes were tearful for my daughter and her best friend. They seemed to hang on to every second together as I went over my checklist for the journey. Finally, the moment came to leave, and we pulled out of the driveway. We were on our way.

Once we got a few miles behind us, our focus began to change. It was as if a fog had been lifted. The emptiness we had felt saying goodbye was replaced with the anticipation of new hellos. Suddenly we could focus on the next step—the actual move into college. On the Auto Train to Florida, we had many uninterrupted hours to spend together and talk about what lay ahead. Steffany even had the chance to meet other young people heading south to various colleges. As we got closer to our final destination, our spirits began to brighten.

Steffany's father joined us at the university and the three of us shopped for appliances and other necessities. We included everything on the college list until our car could carry no more. As the three of us drove onto the university grounds, we joked that we looked like the Beverly Hillbillies arriving in Hollywood.

On campus, the energy was high. So much to do! Like ants on a mission, students and parents hustled around pushing dollies loaded with luggage, boxes, and small appliances. The environment was filled with feelings of excitement, nervousness, hope, and anticipation.

We found ourselves energized about being there and joined the crowds of families spending money in the book store on logo shirts, hats, and bumper stickers. Parents seemed eager to openly chat about their incoming freshman and from where they came.

The Student Center was lively as parents and their freshmen signed up for programs and asked questions. Signs with directions and information were posted everywhere. Crowds also gathered outside the Student Center, where banks offered credit card and cell phone sign-ups.

Once we got Steffany signed in and set up in her dorm, we waited for her roommate to arrive. One half of the dorm room looked warm and inviting while the other side looked bare with mattress and box springs, an empty desk, and bland concrete walls. I could feel Steff's anticipation for meeting her new roomie and knew that she was worried that she might not appear. Finally, the new roommate and family arrived. We visited with the new parents while both girls ran off to get the new roommate registered for her school ID card.

Steff seemed to like her roommate and made friends very quickly with other girls in the hall. I dreaded saying goodbye but felt joy for her obvious excitement and good spirits. Our farewells were quick; I was off to catch a flight, and she was off to catch a bite to eat with her newfound friends. On the plane home, I remember gazing out the window and feeling a sense of relief as I recalled my daughter's smiling face as she ran off with five other freshmen to the dining hall. That vision carried me all the way home. I was pleased to see how well I had done with my saying goodbye. As brave as I felt then, little did I know that the hardest part was yet to come.

For some parents, saying goodbye on move-in day can be more emotional at the farewell. One mother shared her solution:

As parents, we dreaded the move-to-college day and feared the worst of an outpouring of emotions. Due to a large amount of luggage, my husband and I took two cars to move our only child to school. As I look back, this was an unexpected blessing. The emotions seemed to get postponed for the rides both ways. On the long drive to Dickinson College, the focus for me was on the special, uninterrupted visit with my daughter. When the time came to say goodbye, and the

emotions began to erupt, the focus was on a safe drive back.
I was able to put my emotions in neutral, get behind the
steering wheel, and safely drive the long distance home. It
was as I entered the driveway of our house that the emotions
broke loose and my sobbing began!

Steff

The summer before I left for school was so busy it
seemed like a blur. I worked a part-time job but spent
much time with my mother running all kinds of
errands to prepare for college. Mom often got on my
nerves with all of her prodding and scheduling. I had
absolutely no idea of the time, effort, and money that
could go into preparing for college. At times, I realized how far away I was going and how my new life was
not going to provide the usual comfort of home,
familiar school, family, and friends. It was a new
beginning and what seemed so distant and exciting
during my senior year was now more imminent and
somewhat frightening.

I spent most of my time with my high school
friends. We chatted about what we thought college
would be like. By chance, our schools were so different in their sizes and locations. I had chosen a

bigger school that was further away and knew I wouldn't be able to come home as often as I wanted. Again, I tried not to think about that too much and wanted to just let go.

> I'm worried about how many more hours I will have to spend in college on homework compared to the hours I spent during high school.
>
> —Student, Texas

All of a sudden departure day was upon us. For the first time during the busy summer, I stopped, took a breath, and wondered where all the time had gone. All year I had anxiously awaited this day. Now that it was here, I was unsure of how ready I was to face it.

On Our Way

Saying goodbye to my boyfriend and best friend was difficult for me. The morning I left, I didn't know what to think or how to feel. I felt scared, excited, happy, and sad. I wasn't sure if what I was doing was right. Mom and I drove away from home waving to my best friend, who was tearfully sitting on our front step, and my stepfather, who stood beside her. All of us had our own feelings to deal with. I felt numb. I couldn't look back at my house or my girlfriend. I remember burying my head in the pillow that rested on my lap, and crying uncontrollably. This was a different cry because it wasn't the usual "I need comforting" cry. It was an "I'm confused, what do I do? What am I feeling?" cry. And that made me cry even more.

The Arrival on Campus

The arrival on campus brought butterflies to my stomach. As we entered the campus, I felt as one with the car. My face was literally pushed against the glass window because of its full load—suitcases, boxes, clothing, appliances, and pillows.

It was my choice to move on campus as soon as the schedule permitted. I wanted to get the feel of my room, my dorm, and the area. Moving in was a long, exhausting process. There were many trips to the car on that hot August day. Decisions had to be made on the location of personal items, furniture, carpeting, and wall hangings. Mom and I unpacked boxes and bags while Dad set up the appliances. It was a tedious process and I had forgotten how much stuff I had brought.

With coed housing, there can be more tension and competition to impress.
By sophomore year, hopefully, students will get over this.

—Student, Virginia

43

By midafternoon, I was settled into my college home. I had met new faces in my hall but had not yet met my roommate. My fear was that she wouldn't show and I'd be alone. We had talked earlier that summer on the phone. She was kind of quiet and didn't seem as excited as I was and this had worried me. Now, here I was at school, settled, and with no roommate! The other girls in the hall were already buddied up with their new roomies and I was wondering when and *if* mine would ever show up. She finally arrived. I knew my way around at this point and took her under my wing to help her accomplish the procedural part of checking in. This felt good. I came to find out that the two of us were polar opposites in almost every way (schedules, friends, interests). But despite our differences, we felt a need to stick together and we got along fine.

> There is enough opportunity to socialize at parties and many other places outside your dorm. It's really a matter of personal preference. At a coed school, sometimes a single-sex hall can be a nice change of pace.
>
> —Student, Maryland

The departure of my parents was near. It was difficult saying goodbye to them and I tried not to appear

44

upset—just a thank you and a quick unemotional hug. I was worried about Mom crying because I knew that would start me crying. A group of new friends waited for me to join them to the dining hall, so off I went. The truth was, I wanted to run after my parents and yell, "Okay, this was really nice! Now let's go home." But I knew this was it. I had to take control of myself and act like an adult; after all, I was one.

Trap Doors

Tips from Mom for Parents

✳ **Be aware:** Expect and accept emotional eruptions both at the time of your child's departure from home and the time when you drop your child off at college. The departure can be an emotional experience for you as well as your young adult. Tempers can flare or tears can flow. After all, tensions have been building up all summer long in anticipation of this event.

✳ **Read up:** As a parent, go through and read carefully the reams of information sent from the college. Keep a file of this information and don't depend upon your child to read it alone. You will find helpful tips and important directions on schedules, shopping, packing, and move-in that should not be missed.

✳ **Use your resources:** For help in packing, pull from college lists and the advice of others who have gone through the process. A shopping list of college necessities for the freshman year is most helpful while preparing for the move.

Colleges often send these lists with the orientation materials. If you don't have one, ask a parent who has recently sent a child off to school if she has one to lend you. Don't count on your own instincts to know what is needed. It is amazing how much you may not think of!

✳ **Talk about telephone use:** Make sure your student knows the ins and outs of his phone plan's calling zones, text messaging costs, and the number of minutes allotted per month. Cell phone overage charges can add up quickly! Email is an effective and cheap way to keep in touch. If the student doesn't own a computer, he can use the school's computer lab.

✳ **Money matters:** Talk financial responsibilities before the move. It is important to communicate openly with your child on money issues. Decide what the respective responsibilities are for parent and child, and set limits when necessary.

✳ **Meet the Resident Assistant (RA):** On move-in day, it is important to meet the Resident or Hall Assistant. Most dormitories will have a meeting during the orientation program to introduce the floor and RA to the parents. If there are any future concerns regarding your child (health, where-abouts, etc.), this is the person, other than the roommate, who can be contacted. It is not the RA's responsibility to parent your college student, but it is their responsibility to keep an eye out for potential dangers or serious problems.

✳ **Bring and leave the necessary tools:** Several times during the freshman move-in, we wished we had the essential tools: hammer, nails, pliers, hooks, and screwdriver. We had everything else. Bring adhesive hooks for the concrete walls of the dorms, the backs of doors, and inside closets. They are great for holding towels, bathrobes, laundry bags, jackets, hats, and purses. Be sure to leave tools with your students, as they may change their room arrangements from time to time.

Tips from Steff for Students

✳ **Prepare to be emotional:** Saying goodbye to family and friends can be difficult. No one could have prepared me for the feelings I had as I left my best friend and my boyfriend behind. I felt frightened and lost. Allow yourself to feel the sadness of the goodbyes and know that, with time, everything will feel better.

✳ **Speak with your roommate ahead of time:** Call your assigned roommate for an introduction and to discuss how you will share getting the necessities for the room. The college will send you the name and phone number of your assigned roommate. Make contact with her or him. It might feel uncomfortable at first, but it breaks the ice and helps each of you to plan what to bring to the new living quarters.

✳ **Pack light:** I think it is common that students pack three times the clothing they need or will ever use. I was warned of this before I left, and I still managed to bring enough clothing for the whole floor and probably enough shoes for the entire community!

✳ **Leave expensive valuables at home:** Unfortunately, theft can be a reality on campus. Any valuable jewelry, watches, or other valued items should not come to school. Do not forget to lock your dorm door when you are not in the room.

✳ **Consider waiting to buy some of the appliances at school:** Many colleges allow appliance dealers and stores to sell small refrigerators, microwave ovens, and carpeting on school property during check-in day. Prices are reasonable. Compared with bringing these items, this approach can save a lot of time, space, and hassle.

✳ **Pack wisely for long-distance moves:** For those who fly or take the train to college, box and mail some of your items.

✳ **Don't be afraid of coed dorms:** I had the opportunities to live both in single sex and coed environments in college. Eventually, I liked both, although, at first, I found the coed living arrangements a little less comfortable (maybe if I had been raised in a family with brothers, I would have felt differently). The discomfort did not last long, however. After a short while, except for not being able to share clothing and accessories with my male neighbors, everything was the same as in a single-sex dorm. We hung out together, visited each other's rooms, and got along fine. Most of the time, the polite habit of knocking before entering is practiced.

✳ **Getting along with the roommate takes work!** It is hard enough living in a small, shared space with a stranger, but it is important to try to establish trust and a positive relationship with your roommate. There have been roommate horror stories, but you should try to develop a decent relationship for the time you are together. If the two of you find that you are not meant to room together, talk with your RA and see what can be worked out. In my case, my roommate and I made arrangements to switch after the first semester.

✳ **Consider your car options:** I did not have a car on campus during my first year. I missed having access to one but learned how to get around. Most campuses have transport alternatives to get you where you need to go. However, having my car during my sophomore year brought me a new sense of freedom; I could shop, go into the city, and go places on weekends.

Be aware there are some drawbacks to having the car: everyone becomes your friend in order to bum a ride (to the stores, parties, sporting events, airport, bus or train station, you name it) and finding parking on campus can be next to impossible since colleges are very strict in policing parking. If you don't have a designated sticker, you do get tickets! These tickets can keep you from graduating if they are not paid. And gasoline and general upkeep can be costly on a college student's budget. Also, the chances of car dents and damage because of tight parking are quite high.

Chapter 3

The Student at School,
Parent at Home

Doors Apart

The whirlwind of the summer before college is behind us. Two separate doors now exist: the one at home and the one on campus. For parents, the challenge is to adjust to a more stable, yet perhaps too-quiet, home-front. For the young adult, the challenge is to adjust to a more dynamic and unaccustomed habitat. For the entire family, the changes in their environments can produce a variety of emotions.

Home Quiet Home

My own master's studies in social work covered the many stages of the life cycle including the "Launching of Children" stage. At the time of study, I seemed to understand the key principles of this stage enough to write a paper about it. My studies helped me to better understand the empty-nest syndrome in an intellectual sense but did not prepare me personally for what I was about to experience.

Our house now seemed abnormally quiet. The phone didn't ring as much. The familiar sounds of chatter were gone, as were the whispers, the music, and the laughter from my daughter's upstairs room. Any reminders of her that remained—a book bag, her sneakers, her key ring, the yearbook—all brought a heavy feeling to my stomach and tears to my eyes. I actually changed my traffic pattern around the house so that I would not have to walk by her room.

The reality of this emptiness in my life hit me when I went grocery shopping for the first time after Steffany had left home. Suddenly, I was shopping only for my husband and myself. I felt sad as I walked to the aisle of Steff's favorite cereals and sadder as I passed her favorite snacks. There was now no need to add these to my cart so I passed by quickly, but I couldn't hold back my tears. I felt as empty as my cart looked. I finished shopping as quickly as I could, loaded the car, and sobbed all the way home.

Fall, my favorite season, was approaching, but my usual excitement wasn't there. I stayed busy with my work and home projects, but no matter how hard I tried to move on, some emptiness stayed with me morning and night.

September (Journal entry)

I'm tired. I shed some tears as I went in Steff's room tonight and plopped on her bed. It felt so familiar. The room smells of her fragrances and her high school book bag sits on the floor. I thank God for the relationship Steffany and I have and I tell myself that this is a normal stage to go through. This is a big transition for me. I believe I'll get through it fine, but it seems so hard right now.

I continued talking to other parents who were experiencing this phase of life and found that I was not alone. A single mother shared:

I empathize with parents who have found themselves in a house echoing with the memories of days gone by. For me, my career filled my daytime hours but I dreaded coming home to the cold silence of my house.

Another mom sending her youngest child off to college wrote me in an email:

I am still trying to articulate exactly what it is I'm feeling. I feel like I have been hit by a Mack truck! I was not prepared for this emptiness. It is a mixed bag of emotions. I'm happy and proud of where my children are going and what they have accomplished. Yet, I feel sad and alone. I feel guilty and selfish for my emotions of sadness. With my daughter already 2,000 miles away and my son leaving in a few months, I ask myself, What will be my role as Mom?

One couple could not return home after their son's departure:

My wife and I planned a two-week vacation after we checked our only son into college. Neither of us could bear the thought of

coming home to an empty house. When we returned, we closed
his bedroom door because we couldn't look at his unusually neat
and empty room. It remained closed until he returned home for
the holidays.

Steffany's father and I are divorced and although Steffany lived with my husband and me, her father remained supportive and involved in her life. I wondered if he was feeling the same emptiness that I was. I felt a little relieved and more normal when I found that he, too, missed her and found himself phoning her at school often. Hearing this, I did not feel alone in my loneliness.

Not surprisingly, fathers seem to have the most difficulty in understanding and dealing with their emotions toward letting go of this era. Women seem more comfortable sharing their feelings openly with a good friend or family member, while fathers often keep their sadness to themselves. As a father from Maryland shared:

I'm trying to remain a strong shoulder for my wife to cry on when
our little girl leaves for college. My biggest worry, though, is
being strong enough for both her and myself!

A teary-eyed dad from Florida told us:

Knowing that my little girl is leaving home makes me feel that any past control I had as a dad, is now slipping through my fingers. I realize that once she is away, it will never be the same in our household again.

A guidance counselor and father spoke of his difficulty in dealing with his departing son:

I've spent years counseling my students and, at times, their parents and have always known what to say to help them with their emotions. It is now extremely frustrating to me that I can't console myself with my emotions! I am wanting to appear strong for my son and am not sure how much to share with him about my deep feelings.

I'd say being away from home and family impacts me most heavily. After all, I am completely on my own now!

—Student, California

The parent and child often assume they know what each other feels. Too often, both are wrong! In many cases, both the parents and child play the role they *believe* they should to deal with this new shift in the family relationship. Parents don't want to rain on the parade of their offspring's excitement, and the children want to show strong independence. Sometimes, children will actually try to distance themselves from their parents purposely, in fear of closeness being too painful for both.

The danger is that with this inability to discuss true emotions and a change from the normal patterns of behavior, there can be a complete breakdown of communication between parent and child. Strive to be honest, yet not overly emotional. Shedding occasional tears over your child's departure shows him how much he'll be missed.

Siblings, too, feel the absence of their brother or sister when they leave home. There is a shift in the household: an empty chair at the dinner table, an empty bed or vacant bedroom, one less buddy with whom to communicate or family member with whom to compete. In some cases, the younger child at home feels angry toward or abandoned by the older child. In other cases, the younger sibling may feel a new sense of control since there is no longer competition for hierarchy in the family structure.

For all, the realization sets in that one period of family life is now over and a new era involving its own mixture of feelings is on the horizon.

Steff

Away from home...independence! College was nothing like I had expected. Saying goodbye to my parents was not easy. It was like saying farewell to my comfort zone, everything I had known. But once they left, I quickly shifted into my independent gear. Adjustment to life without my parents nearby was easier than I thought. I chose not to dwell on how far I was from home; after all, they were only a phone call away. At times, however, when I felt alone I was a little scared. I knew that all of us, as freshmen, had our own adjustments to make. I could often see the same look in their eyes that I had: the "I'm not sure how to feel" look. Some of my newfound friends admitted it, and I felt comforted that my feelings were quite normal. I met some wonderful people during the first few days and the students on my floor (twenty-nine girls) seemed to get along well. It was certainly an adjustment sharing bathrooms and showers with my new floor mates, but the close living arrangements actually brought us closer together as friends. Together, we would plan floor dinners, decorate our hall for competitions, go out together, celebrate each other's birthdays, and play pranks on each other. My busy schedule kept my mind occupied and helped me to adjust as the days went by.

My roommate and I were very different, personality-wise, but we got along well. We felt comforted by sharing the newness of the environment together. I found other girls on my floor with whom I chose to spend my time as well, and we traveled as a group some-what clinging to each other during the early days of freshman discovery.

> I've grown up in a college town, so I'm already familiar with the atmosphere. I can't say that I'm attached to my parents, so I'm extremely ready to get them off my back.
>
> —Student, Pennsylvania

Still, other students might have a more challenging time getting acquainted and feeling comfortable on their new college campus. It is important to be patient with yourself and try to take the initiative to reach out to new people and even take part in campus activities of interest. A University of Delaware freshman shared her story:

For me, the first semester at a large, public university came as quite a shock. I wasn't prepared for the emotional empti-ness I'd find as I struggled to find my way in a sea of endless students. I had graduated from a small, private high school where my class was more like one, close-knit family. My senior year, I was voted Athlete of the Year and crowned prom queen. I was popular and well liked by my peers and teachers. From my perspective, I was on top of the world! I had expected the same feeling of confidence to carry over into my new college life. Quite the opposite happened. Without the supportive environment I was used to, I felt isolated, frustrated, and insecure. I muddled my way through my freshman year looking for and yearning for new friends, a new niche and a comfortable place to fit in.

It wasn't until my sophomore year that I finally took the initiative to get out and meet people on my own. I realized that new friends weren't going to just show up at my door. I'd have to overcome my reservations and step out to explore some unknown territory. I joined some campus groups and recreational sports teams. I made a point to get to know the girls in my dorm. It took some time, but my efforts were certainly worth it. I began to feel connected and my circles of new friends and activities began to grow.

Orientation

The orientation days were great. Interactive games threw us together and proved to be a good way of getting to meet each other. I found that those who went to orientation were glad they did. Some of the people we met ended up being our best friends. Later, we talked about the famous first impressions we had of each other; some were terribly wrong, some were right on. After the orientation period, the start of classes came as a rude awakening. I think some of us had almost forgotten why we were at school. (You mean, this isn't just one big party?)

Trap Doors

Tips from Mom for Parents

* **Expect the empty nest feeling:** Allow yourself to feel the sadness that you may experience in an emptier house. The empty nest transition is a big event that can stir up deep emotions for many parents. Letting go of the day-to-day role of parenting is not easy. Many years of your life have been focused on parenting at home and a newly quiet household can feel unfamiliar and uncomfortable. It is normal to feel sadness and a sense of loss.

* **Don't burden your student with your own sadness:** An occasional tear is normal. Saying, "I'll miss you when you are gone and am excited for you," is a positive way to be honest and can reassure the child that he or she is appreciated and loved.

* **Grocery shop for your child's favorite items and send care packages:** Sending occasional care packages to your child can help cure your empty feeling at

the grocery store, and cure your child's empty stomach with goodies from home.

If you don't have the time to shop, many colleges have baskets and boxes available to be ordered and delivered to students for special occasions.

✳ **Resurrect your old dreams:** It is your turn! Get involved in something that you have wanted to take part in and previously did not have enough time to do. Go back to school, take a class, play a sport, join a health club, or take up a hobby. In her book *Passages*, Gail Sheehy suggests:

> *It is not through caregiving that a woman looks for a replenishment of purpose in the second half of her life. It is through cultivating talents left half finished, permitting ambitions once piggybacked, becoming aggressive in the service of her own convictions rather than a passive-aggressive party to someone else's.*

✳ **Volunteer your time:** If time allows it, get involved with a community activity or charity to help fill some of the empty spaces on a calendar once filled by your child's activities. If you miss the voices of young ones, volunteer at a youth center or club.

✳ **Don't change your student's bedroom into another room for at least a year:** Despite the desire to want to turn your child's room into an office, artists' loft, or sewing room, the returning college student should still be allowed to feel the welcoming comfort of his or her own space on return visits home (at least for the first year). The rite of passage does not mean losing territorial rights!

Tips from Steff for Parents

✳ **Phases are phases!** "Phase" is a word every parent should get used to, since college students can go through many. Phases today include body piercing, tattooing, and adopting different styles in clothing and behavior. Parents need to recognize that this behavior is almost always a phase; the purple hair will not be purple forever. Parents should express any feelings of concern, but in a balanced way. Silence can be interpreted as approval, and heavy criticism can bring on strong resistance. The more understanding and tactful a parent is in discussing the phase, the more likely it is that it will not stick.

✳ **Try not to put too much pressure on your child regarding specific grade expectations before school starts:** Do communicate that you expect them to do their best. Encourage the student to try to get off to a good start in the new environment but don't be overly critical if initial grades are not quite up to expectations. It is difficult enough to adjust to the new atmosphere, schedules, and college-level classes. Be patient and give your child a little time to settle in before placing any undue pressure on him or her.

Tips from Steff for Students

✳ **Pat yourself on the back for early progress you make:** For some of you, moving away from home might be the hardest adjustment you've had to make. You leave the comfort and security of your own home in exchange for what seems like a two-by-two foot room with a person you have been matched up with by a computer. You are initially unfamiliar with the campus, where classes are, and you are forced to meet people and make new friends. This isn't easy.

✳ **Don't question your actions and decisions too much:** You have been raised with parental supervision and advice for seventeen or eighteen years. Now is the time to learn to test your own instincts about new situations and relationships. You might have a negative gut feeling if you are in an uncomfortable situation. Don't ignore it. It is wise to be extra careful the first few weeks of school, as you do not know all the people around you well (although you may think you do). This is not to say don't trust anyone, but trust your own judgments first, and, in awkward situations, take charge if no one else will.

* **Be patient with your adjustment to your new environment:** Once the busy orientation schedule is over, you are faced with the reality of college: academics; new schedules; new living quarters; a new person sharing your quarters (in most cases); and new pressures along with new freedom. At times, you may feel out of your comfort zone. This is completely normal. Be patient; it takes time to adjust.

* **Take part in the orientation program:** I recommend going through the orientation process. While it may seem silly to some students, you really do meet people you like. (Later, during my sophomore year, I actually chose to work on the orientation staff, which was even more fun!)

* **Beware of procrastination and poor study habits:** It is important not to let yourself form bad study habits in the beginning of school. Many freshmen mess up their first semester because they get so involved in all the non-academic activities around them. It is easy to let academics

become secondary. Students might never have had the chance to oversleep for their eight a.m. class in high school, but in college, it is so easy to roll over and hit the snooze button.

Assignments can fall behind easily, and the consequences can jeopardize your entire semester. It is important to make the effort to stay disciplined through the tough schedule and the unpopular eight a.m. classes. This can help you to develop and ingrain good habits for the semesters to follow.

Much of the motivation behind doing my best in school was my desire to remain right where I was! It wasn't always easy for me to keep up with my assignments but at least I made the effort.

✳ **Get to know your professors or assistants:** In some of my tougher courses, I found it very helpful to ask for help when needed. If it was necessary, I scheduled appointments with my professor or teaching assistant to answer any important questions regarding my studies or assignments. This shows the professor that you are interested in doing your best.

✳ **Watch out for weight gain:** Be aware that during the first semester, weight can sneak up on you. Let's talk about the "freshman fifteen." This is the weight that a student swears he or she will never gain (only to come home after four months to find old high school clothes snug in the hips and pulling at the waist). Could it be the beer? The starchy cafeteria food? The midnight pizza runs? No matter what the reason, many students (male and female) tend to put on some weight.

I swore I would never gain a pound when I left for school. At first, with the excitement of the move and the freshman activity, I lost weight, but it took no time for me to become relaxed and appreciate how good the soft-serve ice cream and the sugary cereals were, and how delicious pizza could taste at two a.m.! All of this led to the reality of weight gain.

I tried several diets, all of which I eventually dropped. It was funny coming home to Mom and telling her my new secrets for weight loss. She just listened, smiled, and kept quiet. I think she knew it was just a phase.

Chapter 4

Communication with Sensitivity
The Screen Door

A screen door allows for an open view, while at the same time affording a degree of privacy. Similarly, communication between parents and their child away at college should permit openness in the expression of viewpoints but, at the same time, it should demonstrate a mutual respect for privacy. Staying in touch with each other is important because without communication, there is no connection, and worry, whether justified or not, can take over. All involved should try to be sensitive in listening to, under-standing, and dealing with special concerns or needs that arise, whether they be from the student, parents, siblings, or friends.

For the happy student adjusting well at school, calls to home can be infrequent. This is not neces-sarily a cause for parents to worry. While parents are naturally curious about what their child is up to, the majority of students are busy getting acclimated to their new home, making new friends and adjusting to new schedules and activities. The fact is that with-out any deliberate malice, they can spend little time thinking about home and they may not appreciate the degree of their parents' normal curiosity.

For the student who is not adjusting well at school, calls to home will probably be made more frequently or, in some cases, rarely or not at all. This circum-stance can bring a challenging period for both parent and child. For the parents at home, it can be terribly disturbing to sense their child is unhappy. It is diffi-cult to judge how we should react to this challenge. As protectors, we want to bring our children home to the safety and security of our nest; in our parent-teacher role, we want to cut the cord and allow our child the opportunity to make it on her own.

For the student away at school, unhappiness can be lonely and frightening and at times, it can lead to depression or illness. There is a sense of embarrassment for some homesick students who fear that Mom or Dad will get upset with their inability to cope with the new environment. This is especially true when the homesick one sees peers adjusting almost flawlessly. No matter what the circumstances are that have created unhappiness, communication between parent and child must remain open, honest, and in balance.

Mom

Staying in Touch

I was fortunate to have a child who was happy at school. Indeed, I was the one suffering. To my surprise, I didn't hear much from Steffany after she left for school. My thoughts were with her every day. I wondered about her classes, activities, new friends, and her overall adjustment to the university. I wanted to call to check on her but kept trying to tell myself that it wasn't right to do this too frequently. After all, I didn't want to clip her fledgling wings of independence! At the same time, I was feeling melancholy about her absence and didn't want her to hear the sadness in my voice. When I would call, she was often busy and unable to talk and would tell me she would call me back. I would actually wait by the phone to receive her returned call and, in some instances, wait for a while before realizing that she had probably become distracted.

On these occasions, I would feel disappointed and somewhat rejected. I tried to tell myself I was pleased that she remained busy, but the reality was that I missed our chats and wondered if our bond was beginning to weaken. At times, I even felt angry. What happened to her commitment to call me back? I knew I would drop anything for her. Why wouldn't she do the same for me? How important was I in her new life? Sometimes I felt worried. Is she all right? What if she is afraid to tell me otherwise?

I had many reflective moments during the absence of our personal contact. I put myself in *my* mother's shoes when I remembered how I, as a busy young career woman, was always on the run. My mother would call, I would be too busy to talk, promise to return the calls, and sometimes let *her* down. I was now living the moments that my mom would warn me about when she would say, "Wait until you are a mother, you will understand." That understanding had finally come.

Now, Steffany was in my younger, active shoes with a life that was full and less accessible to me. I was waiting at home, with a life that sometimes seemed in limbo or suspended. I began to feel powerless, lonesome, and neglected.

After a lot of internal turmoil with weeks of phone tag and abbreviated chats, I called Steffany and openly shared (in tears) that I missed our "visits" and badly needed one. I suddenly felt like the child crying out for the parent. Steffany, taken aback by my emotion, reacted at first with surprise but eventually with empathy and decisiveness.

Together, we set a time for our first, unhurried phone visit since we had been separated. This worked. We both seemed to enjoy our conversation and decided to schedule Sunday afternoons or evenings as our "visiting time." It was not easy for me to admit my feelings to my daughter but I was glad I did it. I tried

> Being on your own is the biggest challenge. You can encounter so many problems and you don't have your parents nearby to help you deal with them!
>
> —Student, Michigan

75

to openly share my needs *without* trying to make her feel guilty.

For the parent of the student who is not adjusting well to his/her new environment there can be different challenges. One mother shared the following about her experience:

Jenny had always been happy and loved high school. Her friends were important and she was busy with many activities. This all changed when she went away to college. She was terribly homesick. She called home two or three times a day. Since many miles separated us, I could only listen and offer advice over the phone. While my heart was breaking for her, I tried to remain strong and to stay upbeat for her, as I knew that she was looking to me to evaluate the situation and help her handle it. I tried to tell her to take one day at a time.

It was painful for me not to be able to help more. I would hang up with a sinking feeling. I would cry. The feeling was so helpless. I found it difficult to focus on my job and life at home. I wanted to go to the college, pull her out, and bring her home to safety with me!

The experience for parents with a clearly unhappy child can be harrowing, particularly if there is a significant geographical separation. It is not easy to assess and understand the situation from a distance. Lacking a clear understanding of the situation, it is difficult to judge whether to jump in and help or let go and hope that the child learns to cope.

Most of the time, with proper support, the unhappy student eventually adjusts to the new environment. The best advice to the parent is to be patient and try to remain calm. Being available to listen to your child properly validates his or her feelings, but you should avoid taking a proactive position too quickly. If the discontent does not go away, setting a time goal will help make the situation more manageable. For example, suggest to your child to try to make it through Thanksgiving so he or she can reevaluate the situation with the support of family and friends. By Thanksgiving vacation, the student has only a few weeks before winter break and the end of the semester. If it is concluded that a change needs to be made, it can be considered at the break between semesters.

> In my opinion, I don't think it really matters if you're a freshman or a sophomore transfer. If you're really unhappy where you are, apply as soon as you can.
>
> —Student, Connecticut

Without question, there are situations when the school is indeed not the right one for your child. Even when this is the case, trying to make it through one year can provide a better opportunity to assess the situation properly and lay the groundwork for a well-considered change.

Communication through the Internet

Oh, the miracles of technology! Once my daughter was online at the university, our communication improved dramatically. Email provided a new way for us to visit even when schedules did not permit a direct conversation. I was updated on her school studies, activities, and social events a couple of times a week. She remained open to sharing her activities with me and most of the time, I was thankful for this. As a certified worrywart, I occasionally would receive an email from her that would have my heart pounding as I read it. Many of these were after Steffany had returned home from social events in the wee hours of the morning. The best consolation for me was that she was home writing them, so I knew she was safe!

One such occasion occurred the morning after Halloween. I remember reading Steff's eyewitness account of an off-campus community costume party involving an unruly crowd in the mall, a police response with tear gas, and a long walk home with three friends at three in the morning. Certainly, if she had shared this with me in person, my facial expressions and my tone of voice would have given away my worry and disapproval. However, through the electronic medium, she felt safe to tell me about the incident without being aware of my mouth hanging open with fear! I was given the chance to calm down before I responded with careful thought.

Communicating through email tends to remove the verbal and nonverbal messages that we can project in person or on the phone. The recipient is not influenced by negative body language or tone of voice. The recipient is also able to read the message more than once to digest and weigh the information before replying. On the other hand, emails can never be altered. Words need to be chosen carefully if an important message is being communicated.

Email served as a form of journaling, too. When Steffany felt down or overwhelmed with school and personal situations, email offered her a chance to share feelings in writing. I responded through this medium with supportive, upbeat messages or quotes. She told me later that she printed some of these messages and put them on her bulletin board as positive reminders or affirmations.

Instant Messaging also provides a convenient form of communication between parent and student. It offers a good chance for a "live" chat. A warning to parents, however—don't bug your child every time you see his name posted on your IM buddy list. Let them reach out to you at their convenience. Most likely, they are working on their studies or conversing with good friends and you might be interrupting their academic or social moments!

Even with all the new ways to communicate, let us not forget the time-tested merits of the U.S. mail! I enjoyed sending cards, letters, and packages to Steffany. Often, I would clip out newspaper articles concerning her old school, local events, and topics of interest and gather them into a large envelope to send at the end of the week. I regularly sent greeting cards and occasionally put together a package of things that I knew she would enjoy.

Steff

Staying in touch

Initially, Mom called fairly often and at the busiest of times for me. Sometimes, I couldn't talk to her at that moment and, unfortunately, forgot to call her right back. At first, I felt she was trying to make me feel guilty for not keeping in touch. I occasionally wondered if she didn't trust me and was checking up on me.

I didn't think much about the effect my leaving home had on my mom until one day when I received an emotional call from her to tell me that she missed our "visits." I was surprised and somewhat uncomfortable at first, but then I realized that she actually missed me, not only as a daughter but as a friend. This gave me a good feeling but I wasn't sure what to do to soothe her pain. I remember apologizing to her and telling her that I understood her feelings. It was a touching experience for me. I really hadn't noticed that I wasn't calling. I was focusing on my life at school. At Mom's suggestion, we scheduled a convenient time that would allow us more time to talk. I liked the idea, too.

I must admit that I loved my freedom at school to come and go as I pleased. I had no curfews and no parents staying up worrying about my whereabouts. When I occasionally got homesick, my instinct was to stay active. I rushed a sorority, ran for student government, sunk myself into my studies, and worked on meeting new people. It might have been some form of escapism for me, but it worked.

I had my low points, however, even though they were not for extended periods of time. On occasions, I would handle them on my own and not mention the problem to Mom for a week or so. At other times, I would need to pick up the phone and hear her voice. Our relationship was definitely changing. Sometimes, I was ready to be independent from her, other times, I was more dependent on her. As I look back, I now understand that this had to be confusing to Mom because the tone of my verbal contacts tended to be erratic.

Communication through the Internet

Email is perhaps the best form of communication ever created! This was my connection to the outside world and it was free. Money can wear thin when you're a college student (no matter what kind of family phone plan you have), so email is a perfect way to stay connected. I was able to stay in touch with my friends who were at various colleges all over the country.

I kept in touch with Mom on email as well. Through this system, I could contact her at *any* hour and fill her in on the happenings of the day or night. I could sit at the computer at four a.m. and type her a long message without waking her up. It doesn't matter what time you transmit, the receiver gets the message on his or her own schedule.

Oddly, with this form of communication, Mom and I seemed to get closer. I was able to share things with her that I wouldn't have shared face-to-face, and surprisingly my mother was pretty cool by the time she responded! I looked forward to her emails as I did her letters and cards.

For some students, running to the mailbox each day is the norm. In a world where electronic devices are everywhere, it is still nice to get old-fashioned mail. There is something special about being able to physically open an envelope or package. The only letdown is finding an empty mailbox. Receiving mail always cheered up my day. Whether it was a note, card, letter, or package, I loved it! My mom and my dad sent things to me on a regular basis. Sometimes

I felt sorry for my roommate, who received less mail. When I mentioned this to Mom, she included an occasional note to my roommate or sent baked goods in a combined package to *both* of us.

FOR BETTER OR FOR WORSE ©2005 Lynn Johnston Productions. Dist. By Universal Press Syndicate. Reprinted with permission. All rights reserved.

Trap Doors

Tips from Mom for Parents

✳ **Stay in touch with your child:** Work out a schedule at least once a week with your son or daughter for phone calls. The new student's schedule is extremely busy with the first semester's activities and adjustments. It is important to plan a day and time convenient for both of you.

As time permits, send notes, cards, and letters. Few students enjoy checking an empty mailbox! Include clippings from the local papers that might interest them and articles regarding their high school and the home community.

✳ **Listen vs. lecture:** There will be times that your student will share experiences that will concern you and may represent behavior that is not up to your view of appropriate behavior or standards. Don't jump into a lecture mode too quickly. Listen. When he or she has shown irresponsibility or made a mistake, provide support and encouragement, not punishment. If your child feels you are reprimanding and looking for perfection, he/she may not be as open and forthright with you.

* **Don't be what counselors call a "helicopter parent."** Don't hover over your child! Give him space. Understand that your child needs to learn how to handle his independence. At this stage, this might be a challenge for parents since we have been at the controls for most of our young one's life. It is time for the child to learn to be in control and responsible for himself. Stay in touch, but absent any warning signs of truly aberrant behavior, start to let go and trust.

* **Use the power of email:** Communicate through email. As mentioned previously, this form of communication can be much more open. It is amazing what your student can and will share with you through this medium. We, as parents, can receive the messages, react, and have time to reflect before responding.

* **Be aware of signals of unusual behavior from your child:** Look for hints of chronic homesickness or persistent avoidance of communication with home on the part of your child. If her behavior is unusual, look to get help through the proper college channels. This topic is further covered in chapter 5.

Tips from Steff for Parents

✻ **On keeping in touch:** Understand all of the things your child has going on. Your student might not call you every day, for a couple of days, or even a week. Because of his busy school schedule, he may have no idea how you are feeling. This is actually a good sign because your child is more than likely adjusting on his own. Don't worry! Hopefully, you have instilled in him a sense of morals and responsible behavior.

Don't question yourself and your childraising techniques at this stage. All you can do is think positively and pat yourself on the back that your child has made it this far. He will do his best. Also understand your child will make some mistakes! Take it easy if he does, as you can do nothing to change what has happened. At these times, be a good listener. Hopefully, if the mistake is not a major one, you can be a listening ear, instead of a lecturing parent.

✻ **Don't call at eight a.m. (especially on weekends):** Your hours are now much different from theirs. Understand and respect the different schedules when you call.

* **Don't embarrass them!** Sometimes a parent's worry can lead to overkill with emotional calls and expressions of concerns (sometimes inappropriately shared with the room-mate). Unless there is an emergency or chance of danger, try to chill and don't overworry.

* **Don't forget the U.S. Mail:** Send things through the mail! Freshmen love to find the mailbox filled with surprises. This keeps them in touch with home. Packages are really appreciated!

Tips from Steff for Students

* **Keep in touch with your parents:** It is difficult realiz-ing how important it is to our parents that we keep in touch. They may worry too much, that's true, but trust that this is based on love and affection. They have little control over what you do while you're at school, so it won't hurt arriving five minutes late to a party or listening to a short lecture from Mom or Dad about making sure you get home safely.

    If you actually listen carefully to what your parents say, you'll find that most of the time, their advice isn't half bad. Although it might have been light years in the past, the chances are that they have been through situations similar to the ones you're experiencing (hard to believe but true).

✴ **Except for emergencies, don't call home after midnight:** Respect your parents' schedules and don't call them at late hours.

✴ **Contact with friends from home:** It is important to maintain your connections with your high school friends from home, but don't overdo it to the point that you are not allowing yourself the chance to meet new friends at college.

WARNING!

Make sure you can lock the keypad of your cell phone when you go out for the evening! More than a couple of times, I received a sleepy and frantic voicemail from Mom saying, "Hey, you just called. Is everything all right?" I would find out later that my call button would get accidentally pushed and it would ring my home at wee hours of the morning! Mom would answer and, unbeknownst to me, hear the voices and partying in the background. This would not only wake her but also worry her until we talked the next day.

Chapter 5

The Challenges Away from Home

Emergency Doors

Watching their young adults venture out on their own can be a new experience for parents. It may be the first time they are not in close proximity to their offspring who are facing new kinds of challenges: missing old friends, striving for new relationships in an unfamiliar setting, coping with sickness or even depression while outside the comforting environment of home. For parents who sense their children's challenges from a distance, there can be unaccustomed feelings of helplessness, worry, and sometimes frustration and anger.

For students facing challenges away at school, being on their own can be frightening. Young adults need to be able to reach out for help when necessary. It can be difficult for them to learn the healthy balance between dependency and personal responsibility.

Dr. Mom

Mom's homemade chicken soup isn't just a meal;
it is the culinary equivalent of a hug.

—*Unknown*

At times, my daughter's challenges created in me a large dose of worry, which I then carried around until I knew that everything was okay. I remember the first call I received from her when she was sick. How powerless I felt! I wanted to be Dr. Mom again: to feel her forehead, take her temperature, tuck her in, and fix her my homemade chicken soup...and I couldn't. She refused to go to the college infirmary. I could only suggest remedies over the phone. With no influence over the situation, my worries grew:

What if she has a serious illness? Her neck is sore, could it be meningitis? Who is going to take care of her? One worry built upon another and I finally called our family doctor to ask for advice. I spent a sleepless night waiting anxiously to hear from Steffany the next day.

When morning finally arrived, I called. My heart was pounding as the phone rang several times with no response. Fear took over. Frantic thoughts raced through my mind: How could I reach her? What if she is too sick to answer her phone? I tried all morning until I finally reached her. I learned that she had visited the infirmary, received the necessary medicine, and was feeling better. I realized, at that moment, that the "control" I should be striving for was over my own fears.

Some situations, of course, are more serious and can develop into real emergencies. One mother shared with me the array of emotions she felt when her daughter became ill with mononucleosis:

It was one of the most difficult times of my life as a parent. We enthusiastically sent our daughter off to her freshman year. On a Friday, three weeks into her arrival, I received a call from her: she felt tired and had swollen glands and a painfully sore throat.

While I worried about her being ill, her dad felt it was simply a case of homesickness. I wanted to believe that he was right, but my instinct told me that she had something serious. I called our local doctor who recognized that the symptoms were those of mononucleosis and she was told to get immediate bed rest.

I sat helplessly at home. By Monday, she had checked herself into the school infirmary where she was tested and found to have mono. She rested for a couple of days and, worried about falling behind in classes, went back to her heavy workload. Her health seemingly got worse. I couldn't sleep at night worrying about her. Finally, I decided to drive five hours to see her.

I was shocked to find my daughter thin and listless. My worry was now joined by guilt for not acting sooner! The decision was immediately made to bring her home where she could get more personal medical attention and rest. I worked out the details with the university's enrollment office that very day while she slept in her room. Bed rest at home was the best prescription and her first semester was delayed.

In this parent's case, getting involved was imperative. Calling the family doctor for guidance helped her and her daughter to assess the possibilities of a more serious illness. With this kind of evidence of a real problem, it is far better to play it safe than to be sorry.

Mom, the Therapist

I remember the concern I felt when I received calls from my child regarding emotional and relationship challenges at school. These were sometimes tearful and could involve her studies, friends, and feelings of being overwhelmed by her schedule or even broader questions about her life and where it was taking her. It was often difficult for me to avoid interrupting to offer my own advice. I tried to listen, ask how she felt it should be handled, and then give my advice. After she had unloaded, I would carry this challenge on my mind until we spoke again. Often, when we did speak again, I found a more positive and back-to-normal child who could barely remember the issue and would tell me I worry too much!

It became clear to me that unloading her emotions on me was cathartic for her and stressful for me. One childcare expert describes this interaction as the child getting into the safety zone. The child's instinct is to pass on the worry to one of the parents. Once the worry is shared with the parent, it relieves the child and puts the worry on the parent's shoulders. This occurs at an early stage of development for our children and can continue through adult life within typical parent-child relationships. Parents themselves need to learn to let go of the worry or it becomes a stressful burden for them to carry. This is easier said than done.

More Serious Emergencies

Along with illness, other serious challenges can develop while the child is away at school. Depression, alcohol and drug abuse, and eating disorders can take over your child's life. The results can be devastating to the child, the parent, and sometimes the entire family. Another mother shared her experience concerning a daughter who had developed a serious eating disorder:

We were frequently in touch with Molly during her first semester away at school. She sounded active and happy. During her visit home for Christmas break, I learned she was suffering from an eating disorder. I had recognized something different about her when she first came home but was not quite sure what it was. She seemed withdrawn and tired and looked thinner in the face, but I thought that the stress of her midterms might be the reason. While home, Molly ate out with her friends most of the time but joined us for our family holiday dinner. I remember seeing her push her food unenthusiastically around the plate, but thought little about it.

One morning, I surprised her as I walked into her room with her clean laundry and found her getting dressed. I was shocked at what I saw! Before me stood a frail skeleton of a once healthy-looking body, that of my own daughter! I sat on her bed and wept. What was she doing this for? Why had I not noticed this until now? Was I a bad mother? What do we do about this? I felt guilt, anger, confusion, and empathy all at the same time. My daughter seemed to resent my troubled reactions.

Molly, active with sports in high school, had always kept an eye on her weight. But I had no idea of the obsession she had acquired once she began to put on some pounds during her first semester away. She also had a painful breakup with her high school sweetheart after the first few weeks of school. I did not realize that all of this could have such a traumatic effect on my daughter.

Unfortunately, her father and I did not initially handle things well. We got angry with Molly, reprimanded her, and generally treated her like a small child. We told her that we were pulling her out of school until she straightened herself out. This created a bigger wedge between us as a family. Finally, through advice from a friend, I contacted a therapist who helped us see things differently.

Though initially against my daughter's wishes, we got profes-sional help as a family. Molly did not return to school in the spring and took a part-time job. It took a year of working *together through family therapy before we began to see positive results. It turned out that there were bigger issues that we, as a family, needed to face. As uncomfortable and painful as this experience was, we grew closer as a family. As I look back on that day during Christmas break, I often wonder whether she would still be alive if I had not walked in on her as I did.*

Another mother shared her harrowing experience when her daughter became involved with drugs during her first year at college:

When my daughter came home in the spring, she was truly a different person. She was no longer the sweet, happy, outgoing young lady she had been when she left. She now had an air of darkness and brooding about her. At first I did not realize what the underlying problem was, nor how severe. She was terribly thin, pale, and had an unusual irritability about her. She seemed like a stranger in our home. I thought that she was exhausted and moody from finishing a tough first year but then discovered that she had become heavily involved in drugs while away at school. It started with smoking marijuana for fun, which became a crutch and perhaps an excuse for her loneliness. As the depression became more pronounced, she reached to methamphetamines to "make her feel better." The combination of pot and speed, along with her low tolerance level, led to severe problems. I didn't know how to deal with this dilemma.

My daughter and I both ended up in therapy. I learned that I had inadvertently contributed to her problem of depression. As a single mom, she had always been number one in my life, and when she went off to college, I felt a desire to hold on tighter in fear of losing her. The cord that once bonded us actually became a rope in a tug of war. I was trying to maintain the status quo while she was trying to move away from me and gain independence. I learned that my lack of trust in her abilities had undermined her self-esteem and her drug use was partly a rebellion against my holding so tightly.

Our family therapy was both a mind- and life-altering experience. We both made it through safely but as I look back, I realize the whole period represented by far the most challenging time of my life.

Both of these cases were emergency situations that required professional help. As parents, we tend to fear the worst. It is important to stay in touch with our children, ask questions, be good listeners and, in a balanced way, remain open and aware of such possibilities. Most times, if trouble is suspected, getting personally involved and finding outside professional help is the best course for a positive outcome.

Steff

The times I perhaps missed my parents the most were when I wasn't feeling well physically or emotionally. I tried not to worry or bother them. I realized there was little they could do from so many miles away. I tried to take good care of myself when feeling under the weather but, at times, was homesick for a cup of Mom's homemade soup, or one of Dad's cheer-up visits. For me, only Mom or Dad could soothe a serious ailment. The first time I felt lousy, I called Mom to ask her advice. I knew I was burning up with fever but had no one nearby to help me. Everything Mom suggested I take, I didn't have! I didn't even have a thermometer to check my temperature. As sick as I felt, the college infirmary was the last place I wanted to go. I was miserable. I finally realized the infirmary was the only place I could get help, so I went, got some medicine, and came back to my room to rest. The next morning I felt much better. I learned that lesson the hard way.

My roommate had a more serious bout with illness. She caught mononucleosis, a.k.a. mono (everyone's nightmare), during the second week of school. She felt terrible and had no energy to do any of the fun freshman activities or go to class. Her problem also caused a bit of a clog in my everyday life. I had to tip-toe around our room, in the dark, with blinds closed in order for her to sleep. I tried not to disturb her, but that was nearly impossible.

She was really sick, and I couldn't do much to help her. The situation became difficult for both of us. She eventually went to the infirmary where she stayed for a few days. Her case proved to be a mild one, and she was soon able to return to her classes.

> The hectic workload, along with staying healthy and in shape, has been the biggest struggle for me. Others seem to be dealing so much better than I am.
>
> —Student, Indiana

Mono is extremely conta-gious (I wasn't worried for myself since I had already had it). Within the next two weeks, two neighboring students came down with it. The advice for those who haven't had it: wash hands often and don't share food or drinks!

Stresses on Campus

The busy life at school can cause havoc to students' physical and mental health. The environment is loaded with all kinds of stresses: challenging school assignments, noisy dorm life, outside activities, and relationship challenges. Too much stress can contribute to illness, and it is important to learn how to guard against being stressed out even while dealing with new situations. When possible, fit in healthy activities such as exercise, walks, or finding a spot for reflection or even a nap. The emphasis during the quiet moments should be on taking time to refocus and relieve tension.

Is the Therapist In?

It was rewarding to find some friends at school supporting me when I was facing minor challenges. However, when my world seemed to really fall apart, the only person I felt safe with was Mom. The first few times I needed her shoulder, it was second nature to simply dial home. Mom was there for me. After the phone call I felt better. As I look back, I think I only wanted to share my frustrations and confusions with someone I could trust and feel safe talking to. Sometimes it was therapeutic for me to share my concerns through email before I went to bed. It was like keeping a personal journal.

Sometimes temporary problems such as worry over a test, a poor grade, or an argument with a friend seemed big to me. Initially, I tended to unload all my concerns and troubles on Mom. Eventually, I learned to sort out the more important problems and tried to deal with the lesser ones on my own.

What I had to learn was that after I unloaded my concerns on Mom, she kept asking how the situation was even after I felt the issue had been resolved. It sometimes got on my nerves and, at times, I regretted sharing some issues with her. There were also times that I did not agree with her advice, especially when she gave it without my asking for it!

My friends, at the same time, seemed to come to me with their problems. In all of the madness of the busy academic life, I felt the pressure of being a good listener and friend-in-need. In this regard, my lesson was to learn to emotionally take care of myself *first* and then help my friends.

Depression

Some situations become very serious, and it is difficult to know how best to deal with them. In my case, one of my best friends started to behave in a different and unusual manner. I was unsure how to handle it. She didn't want to join in normal activities, she stopped going to classes, and she stayed in bed for days. I tried to voice my concern but it seemed to make no difference. I spoke to her roommate but could not engage her in trying to figure out what the problem was. I sensed my friend was going through some form of depression but did not know how to handle it.

I felt tremendous relief when, one day, her concerned parents called me to ask if anything was wrong. They had sensed problems since they had no contact from her and she was not answering her phone. I told them what I knew about the situation and found that she had previously had bouts with depression and perhaps was not taking her prescribed medicine. Quickly, her parents got her the necessary help. She left school for a semester, went home for rest and therapy, and returned much healthier in the spring.

The Lure of New Experiences

Being on our own feels great! With parents absent, what we do, how we do it, and with whom are not immediately questioned. As liberating as this can feel, this new freedom can lead to serious problems.

Let's face it; easy availability of alcohol and drugs is a reality in today's college life. Alcohol is the biggest and most popular drug at college. It doesn't seem to have the stigma of other drugs, and students have fun telling stories with each other about their various drinking experiences. The risks, however, can still be enormously high. Students under the influence of alcohol can jeopardize themselves, their friends, or even complete strangers. There were times I put myself in high-risk situations and was lucky I made it home safely. Recognizing the critical difference between moderate social drinking and excessive drinking is important.

Besides alcohol, there are other drug experiences that can be tempting to the new college student. As a freshman, I became aware of drugs that I had never heard of before. At colleges, there are many drugs available and many ways to get them. Availability, curiosity, and peer pressure can lead to experimentation and actions with serious consequences. The risk of catastrophic problems is high when mixing substances.

Taking Responsibility

Students do need to take responsibility for their own behavior. Thankfully, most college students are using designated drivers much more often than in the past. Within my group of friends, when we would go off campus, we would share the responsibility of being the d.d. for the night.

Without evidence to the contrary, parents should not worry unduly that substance abuse is a problem for their students. College students, in general, get stereotyped as party animals, but I believe that this is overstating the problem. Although alcoholism and drug use do pose serious problems for some students, my friends and I are convinced that this is not a problem for the majority.

As a student, you know that substance abuse might be the cause when fellow students start missing classes, lose motivation, put off personal responsibilities, have significant mood changes, and begin blaming teachers and others for their falling grades. If parents sense it is a possible problem for their own child, they should get involved by talking with their child, to his friends, the resident advisor, or a counselor. If there is trouble, trained professionals are the best source of help. If the child is away at school, look for help and programs in his or her vicinity or even bring the child home to get help.

Safety in Numbers

There were two cases of sexual assault near campus during my freshman and sophomore years. In each case, the girls were walking home intoxicated and alone from parties not far from campus. Although the incidents were off-campus, the college took it seriously and arranged for the local police to speak at the dorms, sororities, and fraternities on safety issues and, as a result, we learned to travel in groups. On any campus at any college, no matter what gender you are, it is safer to be accompanied by someone when walking home from a party, bar, or nearby gathering. My friends and I made it a rule to look out for each other.

Newfound freedom can also bring about inappropriate sexual behavior. Date rape exists. Be aware of the company that you keep. Tell a friend or roommate where you are going and with whom. Take responsibility for yourself.

College represents a new stage in life. The opportunities for new experiences of all kinds will be available. Awareness, common sense, and prudence should all be used when faced with this new freedom of choice.

Trap Doors

Tips from Mom for Parents

❊ **Listen first!** It is difficult not to jump in with quick judgments or advice when our children call for help. It is best to listen carefully, ask questions about how they are feeling, try as best as you can to understand the true nature of their concerns, and, finally, make suggestions. After that, for problems that are not too serious or life-threatening, it is best to try to detach. At this stage of our lives, our children are young adults, and all we can do as parents is to listen and provide our best advice. It is the responsibility of the child to either follow the advice or do otherwise. For most parents, it is finding the right balance in the detaching part that is difficult.

❊ **Know about depression:** Depression is the most common psychological problem among college students today. According to a University of Michigan study, one in seven college students experience some form of depression due to the anxiety, stress, and challenges of college life, and the numbers continue to rise. Parents need to understand the causes of depression as best they can. The stage of development during which the child is separated from the parent may be directly involved with a depressive disorder. Most new college students are away from home for the first time dealing with a variety of stressful factors: hectic schedules and possibly disappointing grades; the threat of losing a scholarship; the breakup of a relationship; rejection from new social groups; and other anxieties. These stresses can cause brief phases of depression and anxiety for college students. Most will cope and, given time, pull themselves out of these phases.

✳ **Look for danger signs:** If there is evidence of problems that appear more serious, intervention by the parents might be necessary. Some more serious signs and symptoms to look for:

  ✳ Sleeping excessively
  ✳ Sleeplessness
  ✳ Missing classes
  ✳ Lack of interest in peers and social activities
  ✳ Extreme weight loss or weight gain
  ✳ Unusual moodiness
  ✳ A marked change in hygiene habits
  ✳ Forced cheerfulness

  If such signs are appearing and dialogue with the student is open, parents can help by encouraging children to take advantage of campus resources. There are good counseling services on most campuses and the counselors know what symptoms to look for and how to treat them. It may be necessary to speak with your child's roommate, friend, or Resident Advisor. This should be done with care and tact. If the information from these outside sources is alarming, share your feelings with your child and, if appropriate, discuss a plan for corrective action.

Tips from Steff for Parents

✻ **Drugs and alcohol *can* affect your child:** It is too easy for parents to take the "not my kid" approach when it comes to thinking about the potential problems of drugs and alcohol at school. Colleges are aware of the problem and do what they can to control it. No matter how strong the school policies, the reality is that alcohol and drugs are available in many forms for underage or of-age college students. Don't be blind to the fact that experimenting does take place. For you, the parent, it is about awareness and communication.

This does not mean to assume the worst without any evidence and to be overly suspicious of your child. It requires a fine balance to do it just right. If you do become convinced there is a problem, you should step in. You might be saving a very important life.

Tips from Steff for Students

✳ **Know the possible repercussions of unloading problems on your parents:** Once you unload your problem on your parents, whether it involves academics, relationships, homesickness, or just being unhappy, they will worry about it even more than you do. Whether we like it or not, our parents take on our problems and it's sometimes difficult for them to let go.

Warning: If you have a boyfriend or girlfriend who hurts you, it can take much longer for your parents to forgive him or her than it will for you (if they ever do forgive).

✳ **Take control of your health:** Sickness spreads easily in college atmospheres, a consequence of the close living quarters and the amount of time people spend together, sharing drinks, food, and space.

The best advice is:

✳ Don't share drinks and food.

✳ Wash your hands often...that's where we pick up most of our germs! (I kept little bottles of disinfectant gel near my bed that I used often).

✳ Get rest. I found this was not always easy in a dorm. Yes, it is noisy twenty-four hours a day, seven days a week and I, too, didn't want to miss out on any action!

❋ Take advantage of free on-campus resources. Use the infirmary when feeling sick. I refused to do this at first but eventually concluded it was the best place I could get some sound medical help away from home.

❋ Talk to your family doctor about getting shots and vaccinations for such illnesses as hepatitis, meningitis, and the flu. Most school infirmaries offer some of these on campus for a small fee.

❋ If you conclude that a friend has a serious problem, don't ignore it. Do something. Use your best judgment communicating this to someone who can help. Depending on circumstances, this could be the Resident Advisor, your friend's parents, a mutual friend, or health professionals. Do not leave the problem unattended—someone suffering from depression or serious emotional problems can make bad decisions that may change or even end his or her life. (It's frightening, but true.)

❋ **Be smart about drugs and alcohol:** In the end, you have to be accountable for your own actions. New freedom can bring the possibility of sampling new experiences. Be very selective in what these will be for you. Do not fall victim to the abuse of drugs and alcohol. There might be opportunities for binge drinking and competitions to out-drink someone else. For most, the accessibility of drugs on campus will be an eye-opener. It is almost certain that in college you might see some things happen that you have never seen before. Some behaviors can be shocking. Just be aware and careful. Try to make the best judgments on whether and how you participate.

When at a social event, bar, or club, never let a stranger pour your beverage. Always keep an eye on your own glass (even when you go to the restroom). Being responsible means not allowing someone to put something lethal or dangerous in your drink. A stranger's sick prank can cause havoc or even death. Be aware that this can happen.

WARNING!
Getting "roofed"

Definition: Having someone slip something foreign into an innocent victim's drink.

True story:

I received a long email from a freshman who is a student at a large university in the south. He was attending a pledge night with a date at one of the fraternities. He continued to grab drinks from the unauthorized bartender during the night and before he knew it, found himself alone, in a convenience store parking lot, miles from the university campus. He was groggy and confused and had no idea how he got there or why. Hours had slipped by. No theft took place and his wallet was still on him, so he took a cab back to his dorm. His date said he walked outside for some air and never returned.

He had amnesia for those passing few hours and can only assume that he was victim of a dangerous prank: getting roofed.

Three lessons came from this:
1. It can happen to anyone—male or female.
2. Keep an eye on your own drink.
3. It can happen on or off of campus.

Chapter 6

Parents' Weekend
The Open Door

The first visit for Mom and Dad on campus places the welcome mat at the child's door. Parents' Weekend is perhaps the first time that parents get to see their young adults since they left for college. This event offers opportunities for the parent to observe campus life in action, meet their offspring's new friends, visit with the school administration, and, importantly, get a firsthand reading on their child's adjustment to the new life. It is also the first time that parents might feel a form of role reversal, with the child assuming more of a leadership role.

Mom

I remember my excitement before Parents' Weekend! I had studied all of the information from the university including the schedule of events, and it looked like a busy two days. I sensed Steffany's excitement about the visit, and this meant a lot to me. We made our reservations early to secure a hotel fairly close to the campus.

For divorced families, the question can arise regarding which parents are going to Parents' Weekend. This can create some tough decisions and discomfort for everyone involved. Make arrangements that are mutually agreeable and, importantly, spare the student from being caught in a no-win situation. In our case, three of us were going to this event: mother, father, and stepfather. Fortunately, we have an amicable relationship, and Steffany seemed happy that all three of us were coming (although not arriving together). The weekend agenda was packed with activities for the parents: meetings, lunch with the college President, a football game, and concerts. My husband and I arrived, checked in, and immediately headed over to the university to see my daughter.

The campus was buzzing with activity as all ages bustled about, many sporting university logo shirts and hats. Parents and grandparents wandered aimlessly around the student center, school store, and dorms as they followed the lead of their confident student children.

I remember going to Steff's dorm room and surprising her. She seemed excited to see me at her door. I glanced in her room: it was disheveled and lived-in, certainly not as neat as on move-in day. At this point in time, I didn't care a bit about her housekeeping! We hurried off to grab a lunch.

It was during this weekend that we got the first inkling of role reversal in our dealings with our daughter. Steffany gladly accepted our offer of lunch and led us across the crowded campus, occasionally stopping to hug friends and make introductions. At the campus restaurant, she directed us to the food line, ordered our lunch choices, collected our tickets, and found us a table. I felt as disoriented as a lost child looking for direction in a shopping mall. The only familiar activity in this experience for us was paying the bill!

Clearly, our daughter had taken charge of the program and we were the guests. During our visit, she guided us confidently about the campus, the adjacent areas, and even the big city outside of the school community. She made the suggestions for dinner, guided us to the local spots, and gave us an exciting taste of nightlife in her new hometown. I watched in amazement as she essentially assumed control of the weekend. We were not unhappy to follow her recommendations. As a parent, I felt proud, but at the same time, somewhat deprived in *my* role.

I noticed that the age of embarrassment of having your parent around was not a factor for us. This pleased me tremendously. Arm and arm, my daughter walked me around campus. I felt that she was proud to have me by her side. I observed Steffany as I had never before. I didn't want her to feel that I was keeping an eye on her, but I felt a wonderful sense of pride as I could see a new level of independence and confidence.

A single mom shared her Parents' Weekend experience when she traveled a distance to visit her daughter:

I had made reservations at a suite-type hotel and invited Amanda to join me for the weekend. To my pleasant surprise, she was delighted. She looked upon this as a mini-vacation, packed a bag, and came and stayed with me the entire weekend. We went to the football game together, ate our meals in the suite, watched movies, and visited like old girlfriends!

On the other hand, don't be surprised if the child's response toward having parents visit does not convey great enthusiasm. The child's need might be to prove independence. Be aware. One disappointed mother shared her memory of visiting her son:

I didn't sense a warm welcome when Tim met me in his dorm lobby. To be outgoing was not his style. However, we hadn't seen each other in months and in my heart I was hoping for more. I was also on my own for most of the weekend as I attended the college functions. Tim didn't want to go to the football game, so I went back to my motel instead of attending it by myself. I took my son out for dinner on the first night but discovered that he had made plans with his friends for the next evening. Being alone as a visitor didn't help matters but not having Tim make himself available for the functions was very disappointing. I'm not sure the decision for me to visit was the right one for either of us, but, as it is, I am sure my disappointment was deeper.

In general, students can have varying degrees of comfort about their parents' campus visit. So much depends on existing family relationships and these should be considered carefully when decisions on the visit are being made. If the student really wants it, and if timing and finances permit, parents should make a strong effort to be there. This weekend is a great opportunity to build on the relationship: parents show pride, trust, and friendship, and students display independence, leadership, and their own pride. At the end of the day, most students appreciate being taken off campus by their parents for a good restaurant meal.

Parents' Weekend is also an opportunity to meet the student's new friends and their parents. In our case, we joined with other families to attend some of the events such as the football game, on-campus activities, and meals. It was nice to exchange observations and experiences with other parents. And to some of our daughter's friends whose parents could not be present for the weekend, we opened the invitation to join us for meals. They seemed to enjoy it; we know we did.

It was hard for me not to notice my son's pigpen of a room at school. Unlike at home, I kept my mouth shut!

—Mom, Florida

Steff

I felt I was adjusting very well to school and was enjoying the surroundings, classes, and friends. I truly looked forward to my parents coming down for Parents' Weekend. It was amusing to us, as students, to see how the school itself was concentrating on doing things to impress the visiting parents: the school grounds were being manicured, paths raked, grass cut, and new shrubbery and flowers added along some of the buildings. We wondered what all the fuss was about until the older students filled us in on the ritual of build-up for the upcoming arrival of parents. After all, colleges and universities live in a competitive world, too.

From the moment I heard the knock at my dorm door, I felt the weekend was going to be a blast. My parents were on *my* turf and it was my responsibility to show them a good time. I was excited to take them to meet my friends.

Mom and I did a few things on our own and had a nice chance to talk. She met me for lunch, a walk, and a workout at the college wellness center. It was nice to have her by my side. We talked like girlfriends; she seemed so interested in my new life. Otherwise, my dad, stepdad, mom, and I attended planned festivities and made the most of the weekend.

The best part was eating meals off campus! Let's talk *eating* out. I accentuate the word "eat" because freshman girls can eat! We shoved appetizers, main courses, and desserts into our mouths. (This may have been the reason for the freshman fifteen pound gain!) My friends and I were thrilled with the flavor and variety of restaurant foods. We were ready for a change in menu from our usual cheap fare: pizza, pasta, and soft-serve ice cream. Believe me, college kids learn the value of the dollar quickly when it is *their* money they are spending. It is special to be taken out to eat!

> The one worry I had about my parents visiting me on campus was that they would try to "parent" me like they did at home.
>
> —Student, Connecticut

As much as I looked forward to having my parents visit, I must admit that I was unsure as to how the weekend might go. Happily, I found that my parents were relaxed and not trying to monopolize my time. I was in charge as they let me plan the days and evenings with no hassles, and introducing my friends to my family went well. After a stressful summer with so many responsibilities being shoved down my throat, this was a pleasant surprise.

The only conflict of the weekend arose after we had finished dinner on Saturday night. It was only just after eleven p.m., and my friends and I were ready to continue the evening. My dad said that he felt it was time to go back to the dorm. To my friends and me, it was early! I was on my turf and had no rules. After Dad dropped us off at the dorm, we went to an off-campus party. The next day, there was a raised eyebrow but no major fuss when Dad found out.

Trap Doors

Tips from Mom for Parents

✳ **Try to attend Parents' Weekend:** If your student wants you to join in on the festivities, and travel costs are reasonable, don't miss this special visit.

✳ **Book your hotel early:** Parents' Weekends are well attended. Book early in order to get conveniently located accommodations.

✳ **During the visit, let your child take a leadership role:** This is the first experience during which I personally felt a degree of role-reversal. The responsibility was on my daughter's shoulders as she planned the weekend, showed us around the area, and introduced us to friends and colleagues. She truly took charge. Suddenly, I was aware of her blossoming maturity. Although it was a new experience for me, it was a positive one. There were moments, however, when I felt a parent's need to control, but I chose, instead, to try to relax and let her be the responsible one. It wasn't always easy, but I actually enjoyed it.

❉ **Get to know your children's college friends:** Everything is geared for the family on this weekend. For those young adults who are alone, it is nice to feel included in family activities. This is also a good opportunity to get to know your child's new friends.

Tips from Steff for Parents

❉ **Make room for your child's friends:** Try to be open-minded about what your child wants to do, and don't be surprised if your student wants to have both your company and the company of friends.

❉ **Understand their hours:** If you go out to dinner, don't be offended if your student wants to go out with his friends afterwards even though you feel he should be ready for bed. Remember, you're on their turf.

❉ **Provide a getaway:** Offer to take your student off-campus for shopping or meals. An invitation to see the world outside the campus is a real treat.

Tips from Steff for Students

* **Plan some personal time with your parents:** Parents' Weekend is full of activities that can be somewhat fast-paced and overwhelming for all, so make sure to schedule some time alone with your parents, *without* your friends.

* **Make things presentable:** Clean up your clothes, try to straighten up your room, and make things as presentable as possible. It is amazing how impressed or shocked parents can be to see organization and neatness!

* **Before your parents' plans are etched in concrete, share your feelings about their attendance:** If you do not want to take part in Parents' Weekend and feel uncomfortable about having them visit, be open with them.

Chapter 7

First Visit Home
The Door Jam

The student's first trip back home is an exciting one for parents and children. Parents look forward to the feeling of a full nest once again; children look forward to a comfortable bed and home-cooked meals.

But along with warm feelings, the visit can bring some challenges. "Home sweet home" can take on new and different definitions for parents and child during this particular visit. Parents expect their children to return automatically to the old set of house rules while the young adult expects to continue his newfound sense of independence. The door jam represents some of the awkward and sometimes difficult circumstances and misunderstandings that can get in the way of a peaceful homecoming. With awareness and open communication from all parties, the return can provide growth for all and be a positive experience.

Mom

The house is alive again!

I counted the days until Steffany's school break. Suddenly, it was here:

December (Journal entry)

As I go to bed tonight, my excitement soars! Steffany is coming home tomorrow morning. I have shopped for her favorite foods and am planning on making her much-loved dishes. Home will seem complete again.

I readied the house for Steffany's arrival; her room was ready and the fridge was full of her favorite foods. I couldn't seem to get to the airport fast enough! I decided to surprise her and meet her inside the airport. I smiled to myself when I saw numerous parents just like me, anxiously awaiting their homebound college children. My heart pounded with anticipation: How will she look? Is she more mature? Is she happy to be coming home? Finally, I saw a mature-looking and confident young woman walking toward me. Our ride home was filled with positive energy as she shared news about college and her friends.

As soon as we got home, the house came alive. An hour didn't go by without the phone ringing. Shortly thereafter, the doorbell was ringing and the stereo was playing. Before the night was over, cars were parked in our driveway and cheerful noise echoed throughout our house. The activity broke the peaceful environment that my husband and I had grown accustomed to during the last few months. At that moment, I didn't mind at all. As a matter of fact, I loved it.

I sent the following to Penny, my good friend and Mother of a college freshman:

Dec. 19
To: Penny@email.address
From: Margo@email.address

Hopefully, this email finds you enjoying your entire family at home as much as I am enjoying mine. The sound of voices, the snacking on munchies and leftovers in the kitchen, the phone ringing, the stereo and MTV playing. . .it is great! Who ever thought I'd say this?

The Tension Begins

Within the first forty-eight hours of Steffany's arrival home, the situation began to lose its initial excitement because of our different schedules, attitudes, and behaviors. Days for my husband and me typically ended at eleven p.m. We normally rose reasonably early for our daily routines. Even in our conservative community, our college freshman's evenings began at eleven p.m., and her need to regain energy meant sleeping until at least noon the next day! It was obvious she did not understand our timetable and we concluded we couldn't support hers.

Soon, I found myself debating with Steffany on her new schedule: the hour she was going out, the time she was coming in, and the ridiculous hour she woke up. I was insistent that her curfew remain at one a.m., as it had been during her high school senior year. "One a.m.? Are you kidding?" She would say, "Mom, I'm now an adult on my own. Please recognize I have no curfew at school!"

Despite each of our headstrong stances, we negotiated to extend the curfew to two a.m. Unfortunately, neither of us was happy with this agreement. I felt I had given at least as much as I could, but my daughter felt it wasn't enough. My challenge was being able to fall asleep before she came home. For those parents who can't fall off into deep slumber until they hear the door open and the keys hit the counter, normal night sleeps are gone. Worse, Steff's late night schedule included weeknights. To college students home from school and *not* working a job, every night is a weekend night.

One frustrated parent, whose freshman son was home for his break, commented:

I was exhausted! I was waiting up for my son and not getting a decent night's sleep. I explained to Dan that I needed him to come home on weeknights by midnight in order for me to have the energy to get up at six a.m. for work. He responded sarcastically,

"Let's get this straight, so what you're telling me is that I have to come in early so you can go to work? Something is wrong here!"

Still another parent shared the story how his son arrived home, dropped off his bags, and moved in to a good friend's house during most of the holiday visit. There, he had no rules to follow and was able to come in and out at all hours with no strings attached. He would come home for occasional changes of clothes and be off again! The parents realized that if they wanted their son to stay at home, they needed to sit down and talk with him to work out a fair set of rules for both parties.

My frustration continued as I noticed our daughter's formerly clean and tidy bedroom take on a new look—explosive! Clothes were strewn everywhere outside of closets and drawers, suitcases unemptied in the corners, bath towels and CDs on the floor, and papers and unrecognizable odds and ends adorning every flat surface. What had college dorm life done to Steffany's housekeeping habits?

Tension at home began to increase. As I waited up for her and watched my bedroom digital clock turning to two-fifteen a.m., as I stepped over the mess in her bedroom to *find* her ringing phone to answer it, as I picked up dirty dishes and trails of empty soda cans throughout the house, and as I found myself whispering and tiptoeing in my *own* household at twelve noon while my daughter still slept, my frustration turned into anger. Sometimes I consoled myself by counting the days until she would be back at school.

I did not like what I was feeling. I was confused and disappointed. I hardly knew this person who had come home from school. Where was life as it used to be here at home? Despite it all, lessons were being learned.

Steff

Coming Home!

With school break approaching, there was definitely something in the air on campus: intense excitement toward everyone's first long visit home. In my case, this meant both the pool and the gym were packed 24-7. As females in a southern school, most of my friends wanted to go home with tans and in-shape tushes. I laughed about it, but I won't lie and tell you I wasn't doing the same thing. This, however, was not so easy considering the extra pounds that college life

> Mom's cooking, sleeping in, and hanging out with my high school friends— what an oasis after finishing midterms!
>
> —Student, New York

had added to our behinds. I was exhausted due to late nights and the stress of final exams. Even though I had little energy at this point, I had not realized how much was involved in prepping to go home!

I had heard how things seem to change when you return home. I was excited to see my parents, eat home-cooked food, and enjoy the comfort and safety of home, but not without a little nervous hesitation about how things would go.

Seeing Old Friends

I was immensely excited to see my old friends from home. I had kept in touch with many on a regular basis and was eager to see how they looked and to share our experiences as freshmen.

I had a ball when I first returned home. A bunch of my friends had gathered at the house, and we sat and gabbed all night about school, weather, sports, friends, and, of course, cute guys and girls. Everyone was so excited to tell their stories about "When I went out...."

or "You'll never guess who I met...." Looking back on it now, it seems funny, because we were all trying to out-do each other's stories. For the moment, it was fun and I felt good about myself.

I was uncomfortable, though, as I heard my old friends talk about their new best friends at college. In a way, I felt a little jealous and betrayed, even though this was somewhat hypocritical of me since I had my own new best friends as well. It felt awkward. Here I was, back with the people with whom I grew up, and something was missing. I felt that we had missed a big part of each other's lives over the past four months.

Tension on the Home Front

As I look back, I probably should have handled my Christmas break differently than I did. At Thanksgiving, the break was only for a few days, but I utilized those days to the fullest extent. There was so much I wanted to do and people that I wanted to see that I made no real quality time for my parents. However, for this short visit, everybody seemed happy enough with events. I felt that Christmas break would allow me more time to visit with my family, but, looking back, I can recognize that my primary focus was on trying to catch up with my old friends.

My absorption in my social life seemed to upset my parents. Both my mom and my dad indicated they would appreciate more time with me. I felt that being home was enough! Mom wanted to do things with me, even run errands with her in the car so we could visit. I certainly did not enjoy running to the cleaners, grocery store, and gas station with her...I *never* enjoyed that. Dad, too, expected time with me but, as it can be after a divorce, time with him was usually spent at a restaurant for dinner or at a movie. This was okay because I would go out with my friends afterwards.

During the extended break, Mom and I seemed to argue about everything: my sleeping late, the condition of my bedroom, dirty dishes in the kitchen sink, not eating meals with the family, poor eating habits and, perhaps above all, my late hours. I couldn't imagine what had gone wrong with Mom. She seemed to expect my schedule to remain as it was when I was in high school.

My parents did not seem to understand that weekends *and* weeknights were for socializing. This, after all, was my vacation. Too many questions were fired at me: "Where are you going?" "What time are you going to be home?" "Who else is going?" "Who's driving?" "Are they responsible?" I would reply to all of these questions with the most common answer among college students, "I don't know!"

These questions irked me considering I had survived well at college for a few months on my *own* schedule, making my *own* plans, and not having to answer to anybody else. I had anticipated that the social life and schedule I had at school would come home with me with the added blessings of no homework, no reason to get up early, plenty of home-cooked meals, and my hometown batch of friends.

To put it mildly, I soon sensed that this wasn't exactly what my parents had in mind. I'll admit that I neglected some of their interests, but I got extremely irked when they asked me so many questions and expected me to follow the old house rules. In my college environment, I was used to being treated as an adult while living independently, and I didn't know how to act as a dependent again. Despite the comforts of home, I started to look forward to being back at school with my own schedule and life.

For the first time in my life, I felt that my mom did not trust me. This was confusing and hurtful to me since she had always trusted me in the past. After several serious arguments and shouting matches, we called a truce and dedicated time to discuss our differences, and how what was going on made each of us feel. This was an important step. I guess we both had some lessons to learn: as the child (guest) in the house, I had to learn to respect the household (my family); Mom, on the other hand, needed to relax more, let go, and trust me.

We've learned over these years that similar issues continue to pop up during each extended visit home. To deal with this, Mom and I have consciously decided to share what is on our minds early and not let the tension build up because of unspoken concerns. We talked during long walks together, or at a favorite place for lunch. We have learned a lot about sharing and managing different viewpoints in a much more constructive and positive manner.

Trap Doors

Tips from Mom for Parents

✳ **Be prepared for your child's independent attitude:**
It's true; our children have been managing their lives and responsibilities on their own schedules at school. Plan to discuss the desired household rules and guidelines with respect to curfews, schedules, and housekeeping early in the first visit home. Be prepared to negotiate. Any person capable of attending college will expect that and deserves it.

✳ **Find time to spend with your child:** When possible, set aside time to spend with family. Whether it is engaging in an activity or sport or having a meal together, this segment of time will give you opportunity to share as a family. Do something you'll all enjoy.

Tips from Steff for Students

* **Understand that rules haven't necessarily changed at home:** Don't be surprised to find that your parents expect you to follow the old house rules when you return home. Be prepared to discuss what they expect. Suggest changes that might help you and be as open-minded as possible.

* **Be prepared for some awkwardness with your old friends from home:** At first, visiting with your hometown friends might seem strange. Each of you has been experiencing a major life transition with distance between you. If you are truly good friends, this awkwardness won't last and will not change your friendship; it just puts it in a different light.

Chapter 8

The Return to College
Doors Apart II

The first extended visit home for the student brings new learnings for both generations. When the child returns to college, the second separation creates new feelings. For parents, it is a return to a quieter, neater, and certainly more worry-free household, and also to the feelings of emptiness felt the first time the child left.

For the student, it is back to class schedules, dining hall meals, campus social activities, and a sense of continuing personal freedom. After revisiting the surroundings of home, the readjustment for the student going back to the campus can sometimes be a little more difficult than expected.

Mom

On the Parent-Child Relationship

There were both joys and challenges during Steffany's Christmas break. Her return home had brought back some of the still familiar atmosphere of life before college: a noisy and active household, more laundry to do and errands to run, meals with the entire family around the table, and the sharing of a family car. But before long, our differing attitudes and priorities began affecting our relationship. At the worst times during her time home, I felt like an interloper in our own household.

Somewhat to my surprise, Steffany's return to college brought back some feelings of emptiness that I had experienced when she first left home. These feelings coincided with a growing appreciation for my own freedom. Steffany was back at college and her room looked bare. The incoming phone calls were minimal. In truth, I missed my daughter's presence in the house, and unavoidably, my household responsibilities as "Mom" were put on hold until the next homecoming.

At the same time, there was a sense of relief that we could have a moratorium in the bickering over house rules and independence issues. I welcomed thoughts of a good night's sleep; there'd be no more waiting up for Steffany's return from late night socializing. There was no question that the visit had brought new challenges to our relationship. Now that Steff was going back, separation would give us a chance to digest and learn from what we had experienced. As we hugged goodbye at the airport, I drew comfort from our unspoken truce. I knew we were at peace despite our recent conflicts. Best of all, our love was strong.

Steff

On Relationships

After only a month at home, I was ready to return to school. My mother had gotten on my nerves by continually trying to impose what I considered were outdated house rules. Although I didn't see as much of my dad, I noticed that he, too, expected me to be flexible in meeting his schedule of events. He didn't seem to notice that some of my priorities had changed. So, returning to school meant regaining personal freedom.

Saying goodbye to Mom was very emotional for me. So much had gone on between us over the break. I hated the conflict. I wanted to go back to my independent life at school, but I wanted her to understand I still loved her.

I had talked on the phone to a few college friends over the break but while at home, my focus was mostly on socializing with my hometown, long-time friends. During this period, I seemed to have slipped effortlessly into my life-before-college role. Separation again from my old friends was sadder than I thought it would be. I also broke up with my high school boyfriend the day before I returned to college. We both realized that we had changed and that the distance between us was too great to allow for a committed relationship. So, with all these factors weighing on me, I returned to school in an emotional state.

Second Semester Blues

Although I was not as fearful as I was when leaving home for my first semester, I was surprised to find myself more homesick in the beginning of my second. Arrival on campus was less event-filled than it was during the freshman orientation period, so I had more time to reflect and think. With my spring schedule starting, I was excited to see new faces and meet the people in my classes. However, I had chosen to return to school early (perhaps too early). It was a gray and rainy day, and my roommate had not yet returned. The dorm hall was silent. I sat alone on my bed, staring at the cold, concrete walls of my room while a thousand thoughts were rushing through my head. Oh, how badly I wanted to crawl into my own bed at home and snuggle with our cat. I now felt alone. It was a peculiar feeling and one that I hadn't felt before. Recent images flashed before me: Mom's teary hug at the airport, my break-up with my boyfriend, my goodbyes to my girlfriends, and not least, memories of my safe and comfortable home. I cried. For the moment, I was not happy to be back at school.

Back to Normal

Once my roommate and other residents returned, I started to feel better. Life in the dorm was noisy and chaotic again and college life seemed back to where it left off. The homesickness gradually wore off. I began to feel a new comfort and confidence as a second-semester freshman. This time, I knew my way around campus and had established friendships to revisit. Missing my family, old friends, and comforts of home quickly faded. My focus was on new classes, activities, and spring. I felt a new energy toward life.

Trap Doors

Tips from Mom for Parents

✳ **Mixed emotions are natural:** Expect to feel some combination of relief and sadness as your child returns to campus. You may feel elated; you may feel sad. Your household will become quieter again and life will seem strange for the moment, but just as life picks up for the student going back, it also picks up for the parent left behind. You may have these feelings each time your child returns to school after an extended break. This is normal. For many families, these feelings are most noticeable during the first year the child is away.

✳ **There might be more challenges for your student on the return to school:** Don't be surprised if your child conveys some signs of homesickness after this first long visit home. Because the second semester of the freshman year is more low-key than the first, there is more opportunity to miss the family, friends, and comforts of home.

Tips from Steff for Students

❊ **Don't go back *too* early:** Anticipate that if you go back early, the campus might seem vacant and inhospitable. If the school is empty, there will be little to do and, in some cases, the dining halls may not yet be open.

Don't be surprised if you feel a mixed bag of emotions about your return. You might feel thrilled to have your freedom back, but at the same time miss the safety and comforts of home much more than you expected.

❊ **Get rest before going back:** Try to be rested for the second semester. Once the normal schedule starts, there is little time to catch up on sleep. Make sure to get enough rest to guard against the colds and flu that run rampant on campus during the winter months.

❊ **Next vacation opportunity...Spring Break!** Going back into second semester can seem like a long stretch of time. There are fewer scheduled activities, events, and holidays to fill the winter schedule. For the student, there is hope and new energy, however, with the thought of spring and the infamous Spring Break on its way!

Need a break?
Did someone say Spring Break?
Break me off a piece of that!

By Steffany

The word "spring" is rarely recognized as the verb that it is, but more often as the season filled with flowers and sunshine. However, come that certain time of year, there is an occasion that celebrates the word in verb format. The word "break"—defined as "To reduce to or separate into pieces suddenly: Smash." I think that these two words basically sum up the whole experience of college Spring Break for many students. It has become a nationally recognized holiday, celebrated largely by a population of students who proceed to carouse, infest, and take over any tropical climate destination that they can get to. There actually should be a cautionary disclaimer placed on every itinerary for Cancun, Acapulco, Negril, South Padre, Daytona, South Beach, and the Bahamas between the dates of March 5–April 25.

People have made small fortunes already on scandalous videos shot during these crazy weeks. If someone could have copyrighted the phrase "Spring Break," they would surely have become a bajillionaire by now.

Spring Break is perfectly wedged between the long winter season and final exams. It is a time of year when students are itching to "let it all hang out" (and most of them do). During this vacation, many students take it upon themselves to lose every ounce of inhibition, common sense, moral fiber, and clothing they may have had prior to this week.

Being a former participant and avid believer in Spring Break for several years, I watched as students of both sexes transformed from well-behaved, law-abiding citizens into hedonistic Neanderthals. There is a common pledge exchanged between most spring breakers and their travel companions which goes something like, "What happens in (Cancun) stays in (Cancun)." I'm sure you've heard it before, maybe even agreed to it. The phrase means it is completely acceptable to forget about any prior obligations one may currently have with anyone or anything back at home. Bed hopping, barside make-out sessions and wet T-shirt contests become common occurrences under this clause. Other than the participants, the influence on these hedonistic happenings and wild activities comes directly from a well-known legal substance—alcohol. Well, mostly.

> Dream big and live a little— it may be your last chance to get by with the excuse, "I'm just a student."
>
> —Graduate from Hawaii

The easy availability and accessibility of alcohol gives all students, underage or not, the opportunity to get plastered during any part of the day. With no scholastic responsibilities to be maintained, many students have been known to wake up face down in the sand, on the side of the road, in someone else's hotel room, or with some strange piercing or tattoo. It's the mornings after that are always the worst.

Some common phrases are "What happened last night?" "Where am I?" "Your name is?" and most popular: "I'm never drinking again." Oh, but you do, again and again. Cure that hangover by chugging another beer. You and hundreds of other students gather around the pool or on the beach and continue to drink away while basking in the sun, leaving a week later with peeling skin and a shriveled liver.

WARNING!

Burnt skin and a hangover are bad enough, but far worse things can happen to careless or reckless students. Spring Break has been a notorious time for serious molestation and harassment, muggings, rape, kidnappings, and even death. This should be another disclaimer placed on all travel itineraries. Students and their parents seem to minimize the risks and dangers prior to planning this vacation. Sure, a parent can forbid their child from going on Spring Break, but that isn't going to help the problem. The only way students can stay out of this trouble is follow these tips:

#1 Be aware of the risks. Do not ignore them.

#2 Keep your head.

#3 Be responsible for yourself.

#4 Look out for one another and honor that commitment. This is the only way to help stop tragedies from taking place.

Choosing whom you travel with is just as important.

Try to make sure they are close friends and not just a random group that you joined through a vacation package. You should go in groups large enough to share responsibilities, but small enough to keep an eye on one another. I have experienced both extremes. The first time, I was traveling with just one friend and we ended up being separated. I found myself surrounded by unfamiliar faces at a large club in a foreign country. Another time, the large group I traveled with didn't realize it had left someone behind until we returned to our hotel, located in the next town.

This doesn't mean Spring Break shouldn't be celebrated; after all, you've worked hard all winter. Just be aware of potential problems and make plans based on that awareness. More preparation needs to go into planning the vacation. Each person going should have an equal part in prepping for the trip. One single person should not be collecting the money, finding hotels, *and* making travel reservations. Map out a game plan for the week. Know the hotel information before you go and get familiar with the immediate geographical area before wandering off and exploring. You might have friends who have demonstrated they are incapable of being responsible. If you travel with them, make sure to keep a close eye on them.

These are some important tips that will maintain some order during the madness and chaos that Spring Break exudes. It is important to follow this advice for your safety and the safety of your companions. These aren't profound thoughts, just organized reminders to not ignore the common sense that exists in all of us…somewhere.

Chapter 9

Life beyond the First Year
Door to the Future

The college years pass by more quickly than you imagine. Like caterpillars, children who leave the safe cocoon of home develop their own kind of wings, which they spread as they prepare to venture out into the world. It's an amazing transformation. The time seems to rush by, leaving both sides asking, "What's next?"

Watching your children mature is an extremely fulfilling experience. Each visit reveals the child's physical, emotional, and social transformation: the boys and girls begin to look like young men and women; conversation between parent and child becomes broader in scope and more interesting; and the personal challenges for the offspring are met with a growing sense of responsibility, independence, and maturity.

Mom

My first awareness of role-reversal was at the university when I was a guest in my daughter's world. As new and somewhat awkward as the change was for me, I worked at trying to let her lead her own life and make her own judgments. As time passed with each semester, I was more aware of the shift in our relationship. Visits home revealed her growing maturity and self-confidence, and I took pride in the change. In reality, I was growing, too.

A New Relationship with My Daughter

Passing time changes a mother and daughter, but not the bond they share.

—*Anonymous*

In most family relationships, there is a point, during the college years, when parents discover a new relationship developing with their offspring. Many of the parents we interviewed shared their own stories about a renewed bond with their children. As children move into adulthood and start to see and experience new aspects of life, both generations find that they have more in common. Mutual respect and understanding grows. Parents learn to listen to advice from their children, and children become willing to learn from and respect the wisdom of their parents.

I remember a particular experience where the sense of this changing relationship became very clear to me. During Steffany's second year of college, she invited me to join her in New York at a career conference she was attending. I was delighted and looked forward to a mother–daughter night together. I accepted and planned to join her for one night. She paid for the hotel on her own and I, in turn, offered to treat her to dinner.

That evening, Steffany asked me to join her at the orientation party. I was rather surprised but certainly complimented that my twenty-year-old wanted the company of her mother at such an event. I felt that to a degree, Steffany wanted my support. At the same time, she wanted to demonstrate her own initiative and independence. She asked me *not* to tell the attendees that I was her mother; instead, she suggested I pretend to be a graduate student or teacher. I smiled, thinking about her growing self-reliance. So, for the occasion, I joined her incognito.

At the event, I did not want to lie about my identity, so I played a wallflower, avoided conversation, and stood back to watch the activity. This had its own rewards. I was touched as I watched my daughter confidently move about the room, introducing herself, taking control of the moment but occasionally checking back with me to see if *I* was all right. Perhaps there was also a touch on her part of, "Am I doing okay?"

Roles shifted again later when I took Steffany to dinner. I was the one in *my* comfort zone as I took her under my wing to a favorite restaurant of mine. The evening brought a potpourri of emotions for both of us as we laughed, cried, asked questions of each other, and shared stories and bits of wisdom. We behaved like good friends catching up on each other's lives. I remember her eyes lighting up when I described my experiences at an age not much different from her own. After dinner, we returned to the hotel and stayed up until the wee hours chatting like girlfriends at a teenage sleepover.

The next day, I left with a sense of comfort, realizing that a more adult relationship between us was developing. I felt she showed more confidence in her decisions while developing a readiness to discuss things with me. I was beginning to see my child's transformation and was pleased at what I was seeing. In my heart, I also knew that my efforts to let go were helping.

A college student from Columbus, Ohio, shared a touching story about her newfound relationship with her father:

My mom and dad have been divorced for years. When I was home from college, I would stay mostly with my mom for the visits. On occasion, I would see Dad when he would stop by at the university on business trips. We would have lunch or dinner together, sometimes catch a movie and he'd bring me back to my dorm.

The summer of my junior year, Dad asked if I would like to spend a week camping with him on vacation. At first, I thought that I would be terribly bored. "After all, what do we have in common?"

Something inside told me to do it. It was one of the best vacations of my life! Dad and I had time to talk in the car, on the trails, and around the campfire. We talked about things we had never talked about before! I even remember one night studying the stars and discussing the constellations. I recall thinking to myself, "How many of my friends get to have an opportunity like this with their dad?" This was the best opportunity for both of us to really get to know each other. I will never forget this experience!

The First Apartment

Steffany's junior year brought her the challenge and excitement of moving out of the dorm. I worried about her living off-campus and out of the safety net of the university. She and her roommate shopped with a real estate broker, found a place to call home, and then searched for a third roommate to make it affordable. This was another step in their maturing process.

Steffany's father cosigned for legal reasons and my responsibility was to help her furnish the new home on a limited budget. Both her roommate's mother and I visited and found mixed pleasures playing cleaners, decorators, and advisors. Our biggest concern was safety, and we felt relieved that the apartment was equipped with double locks and an alarm system. For us, the visit was physically exhausting but great fun.

There can be challenges in living off-campus that do not exist on campus. Good landlords can be hard to find. More common are cotenants who don't obey house rules, don't pay their share of bills on a timely basis, and have unusual living habits. Additionally, expenses always turn out to be more than originally budgeted. If the mix of tenants is a good one, each will realize their responsibilities and fulfill them. In this case, living off-campus can be a fun learning experience.

As the predesignated manager of the apartment, Steffany found she had her own challenges. The toughest was asking one of the apartmentmates to move out. He was not abiding by some of the agreed-on rules and had brought in a significant other to live rent-free. Steffany, as the cosigner of the lease, but also a good friend of the cotenant, had to face up to the responsibility of asking him to leave. She did just that, and it all worked out better than she had imagined. For Steffany, it was another step in learning how to make decisions and take responsibility. Welcome to life.

Another mother shared details of a disastrous housing arrangement that her daughter had entered into:

Carol wanted to move into an apartment during her junior year. She told me that she wanted to be more independent and had found a cute house off-campus. I went to visit and was mortified. It was in what I considered an unsafe part of town, too small for three roommates, and needed a lot of attention. Despite my concerned and adverse comments, my daughter was determined to move in. I finally decided to keep quiet. Her first week was spent with no water supply, which meant no toilet facilities of any kind.

Her roommates, whom she thought she knew, turned out to be heavy smokers and had constant visitors coming and going. Despite her complaints, nothing changed. Carol became miserable and eventually "third person out" in the apartment. Unfortunately, because of her scholarship requirements, she had to stay put through the rest of the school year. The situation became a small nightmare but one she had to endure.

Lessons in Life after College

For some students close to graduation, the approaching responsibility of being on their own in the world outside of college can be intimidating. A recent study by Arthur Levine of Columbia University indicates that a significant percentage of college students are concerned about being able to cope with today's world. To a large extent, their fears are caused by increasing pressures in society as well as expectations and judgments from parents and peers. Additionally, the fast-moving, technology-driven world is, in many ways, more challenging than it used to be.

Today, many students return home after graduation unsure of what they want to do. Parents want to feel that their off-spring are ready to be on their own. They want to believe that their young ones have a good sense of what the world is about and the ambition to succeed in it. Sometimes they miss signs of apprehension in their children.

> I'm scared to death of what's next.
> —Student, Florida

The reality is that life out there for the new grad-uate can be intimidating. So, while encouraging their move toward independence, parents should pay continuing and careful attention to what is going on inside the minds of our young adults. For some time, they may need a supportive sounding board for their evolving thoughts and feelings.

Steff

A New Relationship with My Parents

As the college years advanced, I began to notice a different relationship developing with both my mom and dad. In some ways, our relationships seemed to grow closer—we became better at understanding each other. I hadn't realized how much I had matured during my college years, but I felt that they had. Mom and Dad would compliment me for taking increasing responsibility for matters in my life. That made me feel good. Our communication became more open and direct. The change didn't come as an epiphany; it was something that happened that I started to appreciate over time.

Although Dad and I had our moments of misunderstandings, he kept pretty cool through it all. My relationship with my mother seemed to involve the biggest roller coaster of emotions. She tended to be the one with whom I would lash out or let go. Fortunately, for us, there was the deep mother-daughter bond that had always seemed to be present.

With Mom, our understanding and tolerance for each other's idiosyncrasies in communication grew with efforts on both our parts. Freshman year could be described as a push-pull year for us. At one moment, I was pushing my mother away and at another, I was pulling her close again. I felt she was doing the same. I believe this was subconscious and normal on our parts.

Mom, too, seemed to be changing through this period. She seemed to trust my decisions and was more relaxed about her involvement in my life. She worried about me and still does! I can hear her saying repeatedly, "When you're a mother, you'll understand." Well, I'm not a mother and I don't understand the nuances of her maternal feelings. I do know that despite our differences, I have grown to respect her even more and I work hard to try to validate the feelings and opinions she wants to express to me.

The First Apartment

After two years of living on campus with a group of males and females in a dorm environment, an apartment seemed to be the appropriate next step. I was ready for some peace and quiet and a private bath and bedroom. It suddenly seemed like the right idea to move off campus. My dorm roommate and I discussed the idea, talked to another good friend, and decided to apartment hunt. I felt so grown up, meeting with a real estate broker, looking at places, discussing rents, and trying to find that "perfect fit." Of course, we discussed this with our parents. My dad guided us through this whole process and actually came down south to help us work out the business details for the rental. My two roomies and I now felt that we were ready to set up house!

We realized, of course, that with the excitement of this new adventure came a whole new set of responsibilities: paying bills and a monthly lease! Things seemed to be moving in the right direction until our third roommate decided at the last minute that she could not afford the costs. Frantically, we had to race against the clock to fill the extra bedroom! My dorm roommate and I passed the word through friends, made phone calls, posted ads on the campus billboards, and finally found an extra renter.

The drama behind us, our moms came to help us move and decorate our new home. We did it! We were living in our own place! The sense of independence that I felt away at college now took on a very different aspect. I realized that I was one foot into the next phase of my life ahead.

This new venture brought a variety of challenges: relationship conflicts among the three of us; coping with getting landlord attention to minor problems that developed; and bills, bills, bills that exceeded our budgets! We were forced to develop a different code of responsibilities. As an example, living in the dorm, I wasn't diligent about turning off the TV or lights when I left my room. The electricity charge was included with tuition. Living off-campus and paying utility bills, I soon learned to practice resource conservation. Our food shopping seemed to cost a fortune. Transportation costs increased since I now had to pay for an off-campus parking pass and used more gas driving to classes every day.

Despite our enthusiastic and friendly start, relationship challenges arose among us. I spoke up about the kitchen mess since I seemed to be cleaning it most of the time. My roommates had their own set of grievances. What we all learned was that apartments can provide a pleasant change from the relatively crowded conditions of the dorm but there are new responsibilities to be accepted.

I had a few different roommates in my years in this same house and found that it can be a challenge to live with others who have different personalities and habits. My dorm roommate (a.k.a, best friend) was in the house with me from the beginning despite the warnings, "Don't live with your best friend, it will ruin your relationship." We got along fine. Inevitably, we concluded that it was the third roommate who became a problem.

The apartment was located in a very active area where we could walk to the neighboring restaurants, bars, and stores. We often left our door unlocked for all to come and go freely. Unfortunately, one day, someone took advantage of the "open door policy" and robbed us of valuable possessions: jewelry, computers, and stereo equipment. It ended up a very expensive and frightening lesson!

Changing up the Routine

After being away at school for a couple of years, you get comfortable with your surroundings. The college environment becomes home, and trips to the family home become less frequent. It is not uncommon to want to stay near campus for the summer break or go elsewhere for the holidays. Boys get girlfriends, girls get boyfriends, and old routines fade. With the definition of "home" changing, this can be a challenging time for families.

One student, for example, had a serious boyfriend whom she chose to visit for the holiday season. Her parents were quite hurt and put the pressure on her to come home. Feeling guilty, she changed her plans and went home to her family. She was miserable. During her stay, however, her parents surprised her with an arranged visit from her boyfriend. In this case, understanding, open-mindedness, and a little negotiation helped ease the pain.

Changing Focus on Studies

Many high school seniors don't have a clear idea of what they want to study in college. To those who have a career path mapped out and a passion to follow through, congratulations. This is rare. Statistics show that a large number of students change their majors at least once over the four years of college. I was a double major and changed my second major during my junior year and found that there were additional credits I would have to make up in order to graduate. Fortunately, my parents supported my changing interests.

According to my college friends, parents aren't always so understanding about changes in interests. One friend of mine who was burned out and confused over career choices due to three tough years of studies wanted to take a semester off to work and collect his thoughts about future ambitions. His parents were very closed-minded about what they regarded as needless procrastination. They asked him to leave the home. This led to depression and other challenges for my friend and he dropped out of college altogether.

Parents should be aware that uncertainty over career choices is not uncommon during junior and senior years. Many college students have changed their majors up to three times in order to find what they wanted to do long-term. Despite the complications of changing majors, it is a mistake to be stuck in courses that do not fit career interests. Sadly, there is a tendency for some students to bail out and go through the motions just to get through school.

Lessons in Life after College

The main focus for the college freshman should be on school and the focus for the college senior should be on preparation for life after school. Increasingly, seniors are pondering a mixture of important questions: Did I really make the right choice on what I want to do? Can I find a decent job? Will I succeed at my job? Can I make enough money to support myself in the lifestyle I desire? Will I be happy with what I choose?

The roles and attitudes of women have particularly changed over the years. More and more, women are having to find the right balance between work and family. This may impact their decision on career field or jobs chosen.

Finding a life beyond college can be frightening. There are many decisions and many unknowns. Despite the fears, you need to start preparing. The real world approaches quickly in the last year of college and the senior can either embrace the prospect or try to hide from it. Eventually, the real world outside the college campus will find us all.

Trap Doors

Tips from Mom for Parents

* **Enjoy and trust:** Step back and enjoy the growth in maturity and independence of your child. Unless he makes repeated mistakes in judgment, learn to trust his decisions.

* **Be flexible about majors:** Understand that there might be logical changes in your child's interest in majors. Listen to her thoughts carefully and help guide her through the process. Be patient and as open-minded as possible.

* **Take part in the move to the first off-campus home:** Get involved with your offspring's first apartment or house off-campus. They will need your enthusiasm, support, and help more than in the managed atmosphere of the dorm.

* **Understand that visits home for your student might become less frequent:** As your student becomes more comfortable in his environment at school, he may choose to spend more time there. Try to understand, and certainly work at negotiating visits during the holidays.

Tips from Steff for Parents

✳ **Be supportive, yet open about majors:** With the right approach, you can be an important influence on your child's choice of major. It is helpful to suggest possibilities based on your special insight into their interests and capabilities, but recognize that in the end, the choice should be the student's. Following in a parent's footsteps is not uncommon, but also recognize that it might result from a subconscious desire to please the parents.

People of college age today probably have a much broader view of the world and its opportunities than their parents did at the same age. During the college years, understand that your child's interests and sense of priorities are evolving. Try to be open-minded to listening, discussing, and offering opinions when asked (or if you judge the time is right).

Tips from Steff for Students

✳ **Share the legal responsibility for leases:** I strongly recommend that you or your parents do not solely sign on the lease. My dad signed our lease thinking it would be easier to have the roommates send him the checks. Regrettably, not all of the renters "remembered" to pay him on time. In one case, one of the renters took off for two months and paid nothing. I was stuck paying double rent while she skipped town!

❊ **Keep household communication open:** If early relationships are not working well in apartment arrangements, someone should step up to communicate and encourage discussion of what needs to change. Whether everyone starts out as friends or strangers, this can be tough. It does need to be done, however.

❊ **Watch out for shared phone lines:** I wish I had put a long distance block on my phone line in the apartment. One of my roommates ran up a huge phone bill on my private line while I was home visiting my parents. These calls happened to be to Europe, which resulted in a $600.00 bill that I got stuck with!

❊ **Don't let your guard down on security issues!** Off campus, you have to be even more responsible! Forget the open door policy. Lock up. There is always a risk of theft or other dangers. Don't be cavalier about handing copies of your keys to your friends. Make wise choices.

❊ **Choose a path you'll love:** It is important to try to choose a field about which you can feel passionate. Recognize that your feelings may change during your years at college. Earning power is important, but disliking what you will do day after day can make life miserable. Try hard to find the right choice.

Chapter 10

Study Abroad
Door to the World

Studying abroad is a valuable experience for college students. Travel provides adventure, confidence, and the opportunity to perfect a second language. In addition, it helps students develop better cross-cultural understanding. In an increasingly global business world, a study abroad program can also lend a hand with the impending job search. More than ever, American students recognize the importance of study abroad in a globally interdependent world. According to the Institute of International Education (IIE), increasing numbers show that American students are continuing to reach out to the rest of the world, to experience other cultures first-hand, and to become more engaged in international affairs.

> What better way is there to study art history than being there? Seeing original art in the places it originated, up close and personal, was awesome!
>
> —Student, Pennsylvania

Still, only a small proportion of overall U.S. students take the opportunity to study outside the states. Fortunately, the IIE, the government, and other sponsors are working to reduce the financial hurdles in order to open the opportunity to more of the student population. Many colleges and universities offer financial packages and options with their study abroad programs. And for the curriculum, in some cases, grades and credits can transfer effortlessly.

If your child's school does not sponsor such a study abroad program, they might have an agreement with other schools and providers of abroad studies. Even given parental support, the ultimate decision to study outside the U.S. should be something that your child embraces on her own. Given the challenges and distances involved, a child unconvinced of the potential benefits could have a depressing and, at worst, hurtful semester.

Mom

As a college student, my father wanted me to go abroad with my Spanish studies. Unfortunately, I chose not to apply because my boyfriend and social life remained at the university. Looking back, I have always regretted that decision in my life!

Accordingly, I felt great joy when Steff, finishing her sophomore year, approached me about a summer study abroad interest. Her choice was to study in Spain, since she had taken four years of high school Spanish classes. We researched programs at her university as well as offerings in our own state university. Although both schools offered excellent summer study abroad curriculums, we chose to do the program here in our home state for the convenience as well as the financial savings. It was an excellent choice. Through my daughter, I had a chance to live the study abroad experience that I had long dreamed of!

¡Listo! (Ready)

All of the paper work, travel documents, and university forms were done. The big duffle was packed, the pocket English-Spanish dictionaries and itineraries in our possession, and the passport and airline tickets in Steff's hands. I remember the excitement as I drove

Steffany to meet her university travel group for their departure. She was once again in a situation where she was joining a group of total strangers. So, there was no surprise to me that for her, there was some nervousness and last minute trepidation.

The parking lot was lively with other young adults hugging their families and piling luggage on the bus. We parked and sat for a few moments in silence observing the activity. Steff was carefully studying all her travel companions as they arrived. I, too, watched the other parents dropping off their students for the journey, already feeling a bond with them, knowing that I was not alone in my enthusiasm. We went over last minute details and, of course, parent-to-child advice, and then she, too, climbed on the bus full of anxious young travelers. I watched as the bus headed off and then drove home with joy in my heart and a tear in my eye.

Communication

Steffany was staying with a Spanish family in Granada and, although I had the address and phone numbers, our decision was to stay in touch through email. Every morning, I would go to my computer hoping to read about her adventures. I was ecstatic when I received her first email:

To: Mom@email.address
From: Steff@email.address

Hola Mama,

We're sitting here in this Internet cafe, in the middle of the city. Our schedule is full. We are all so very tired. Have visited places outside of Granada and am going out at night. Lots to see. I like the new friends I have made on this trip. My classes are all in Spanish, so I will be learning faster than I realized!

I am happy so far with my family and living arrangements. Anna, my "mother," does not speak any English and I am trying to communicate the best I can! She is adorable! The weather is perfect. Except for the smoking allowed in the cafes, (a guy is blowing non-filtered smoke in my face as I type.....), I love being here. Will keep in touch. Please fill me in on what is going on back home.

Love,
Tu hija (Your daughter)

To: Steff@email.address
From: Mom@email.address

Hola,
I can't tell you how much I look forward to visiting with you through our emails! It is almost as if I am taking the trip with you. I pinch myself that you are really living the Spanish life! What an experience. Glad you like your friends. Just be yourself, be safe, be willing to learn, and take in the moments and enjoy!

Stay in touch.
Love,
Mom

Time went fast for all of us. Steff's emails became more infrequent as she got more acclimated. I still continued to check every morning. I worried when several days went by without a message from her. Feeling I had no control from so far away was taxing for me. Once again, my lesson was to let go and trust.

One time, I caved in and called her family to see that she was doing fine. My heart pounded as I listened to the ringing on the other end; Could I handle my Spanish language? Would she be there to chat? All was fine and once I heard my daughter's excited voice, I felt much better.

If Steff had a personal or school-related challenge and needed to ask for advice or simply vent, she would write me. Often, I purposely delayed my response until after she had dealt with her challenge on her own. I knew that this experience would open her eyes to the world outside of college and give her another true opportunity to be responsible for herself. I fully trusted that she would grow as a person.

One such incident involved a disagreement between Steff and one of the university chaperones. One morning, Steff overslept and missed the group's tour bus. On her own, she went to the local bus station and took a bus to meet the rest of the group. The group chaperon reprimanded her for being late and warned that she would be sent back to the States if she did not abide by the schedule. Steff wrote me expressing her feelings of frustration and anger. My parental advice was: "Understand that rules _must_ be followed for the safety of each of the students— especially in a foreign country." I suggested that she buy an alarm clock and take more responsibility for on-time arrivals and stay with the group.

By the time she received my email, the issue had been resolved on its own.

A Connecticut family who sent their daughter off to study in Costa Rica shared:

Erin had looked forward to her summer study abroad program for months. She is a very social child who also enjoys her own company and does not need to travel with groups. So, it did not surprise us that she was taking off for a program in a foreign location, knowing no one.

When her departure day came, we were shocked to see a fearful, sobbing side of her saying that she did not want to go! It was difficult for her father and me to send her off in such a depressed state! Within a short time, however, we noticed the confident Erin back to normal. We now laugh at the about face she pulled, when she was due to come back to the States, and cried to leave Costa Rica!

She is taking off for another program this summer to Europe. The study abroad experience definitely laid the groundwork for our daughter to have more confidence in travel and in life itself.

For those who are interested, studying abroad is a great opportunity while the student is in college. The price is usually manageable, the experience is fulfilling and educational, and the trip may help open doors in the student's future.

A student who studied in London told us:

Hands down, studying abroad was the best experience in all of my college years! I learned about other cultures, European history, and politics. I also learned more about myself. And I had fun!

Steff

Seeing other cultures and exploring new places have long been important to me. I studied abroad during the summer of my junior year. I applied through the university of my home state, which made me eligible for in-state tuition. Great for the pocketbook, it also meant I didn't know a soul going on the trip! Mom dropped me off to join the group for the bus ride to JFK (a memorable, hot, four-hour bus ride with no air conditioning and a flat tire). There was some joking speculation that this was designed to prepare us for travel conditions in our new host country! By the time we reached the airport, I had sweated out most of my own fears! We met the rest of the group at the airport and began our journey.

We arrived in Madrid early in the morning and were staying there for a week in a hotel before we jetted off to our living quarters in Granada. This week was important for me in getting to know everyone. We visited museums, monuments, and of course the nightlife scene. After a week settling in there, it was with some trepidation that we traveled by bus to another city to live in someone else's home.

La Familia (The Family)

We were living with families, and I was nervous over what to expect; the food, the rules, the family—and the fact they spoke no English. When the bus arrived, I stared out the window at all the heads of the households waiting for us and suddenly felt an anxiety attack coming on. When we finally unloaded the bus, we stood there in a group as they called off our names one by one. It made me feel like a puppy in the pound. "Pick me, pick me!"

My closest newfound friend's name was called immediately, so my last line of safety was taken away from me. I felt extremely vulnerable; I was one of the last ones to be called. I had barely gotten to know my roommate, so it was hard to voice any of my concerns with her. My worry was needless, given what we found when we arrived at our home; the place was adorable, an apartment building which seemed to be located pretty centrally. I was glad our hosts spoke no English, because this would help me practice my foreign language and dialect. (I only ran into problems when I was trying to explain the more abstract things, like politics, which are hard enough for me to understand in my native tongue!)

Since I was staying in a smaller city, most destinations were in walking distance. The first few nights after school, I headed out to get to know the area. It was really cool exploring new spots, good restaurants, and great shops, and with some guidance from our hosts, security was never an issue.

Food Issues

We filled out forms before we were matched with families. I had marked "picky eater" on my form and, although my madre was very accommodating, I was not crazy about some of the deep-fried food. I wasn't a fan of most of the authentic dishes, and walking by the butcher's shop with hanging pigs in the window didn't help on my food crusade. I relied often on a diet of fried eggs, potato chips, cheese, and figs. Oh, and of course, sangria.

Some nights we ate out and enjoyed being on our own with others in the group. Handling money was definitely an issue, as we all tried to do the conversions in our heads. Most restaurants and tapas bars included the tip in the bill when dining out. I was told the best conversion rate was obtained by the use of a credit card, which was fine, but this often helped me lose track of exactly how much I was spending.

One of the funniest and most memorable food stories came from a student from Gettysburg College who also studied in Spain:

I wanted to cook my family an authentic and traditional American Thanksgiving dinner. For my Spanish "mother," I made a list (in Spanish) of what was needed: turkey, bread, cranberry sauce, etc. I had never actually cooked a turkey before and figured that it couldn't be very difficult! I called my mom long distance to get some tips on basting and cooking.

I was rather confident until the doorbell rang and I was greeted with the delivery of a fully feathered, all appendage-connected, eighteen-pound turkey! It came complete with everything but the "gobble gobble." Mortified, I wanted to run to my room and weep. Most importantly, though, I did not want to offend the ever so excited and grateful family with whom I was staying. I turned to the poor, lifeless turkey, closed my eyes and said "Off with your head!" The procedure was far more challenging than I ever imagined.

Nevertheless, I plucked, cleaned, and cooked the bird and created one of the best-tasting Thanksgiving dinners ever!

Following the Rules

I try to be responsible for myself, but sometimes I can do stupid stuff. One morning, I overslept. I will admit that I had been out socializing with some of our group the night before. When I raced to the location of our university bus, it had gone. I was left alone in the middle of Seville! (This was not the city where we were living, so I had no idea where I was.) I was angry that they had left me. I decided to try to get to the next city on our agenda on my own and, in my broken Spanish, bought a bus ticket and got there.

I was proud of myself as I found and joined our group. Unfortunately, my chaperone didn't seem to share my sentiments since this wasn't the first time I had missed a side trip. I got lectured and warned that, if it happened again, I might get sent back to the States. I was not happy with this response, but I swallowed my pride, apologized, promised to be on time in the future, and fortunately was allowed to stay.

On Your Own

The schedule set by the university permitted us to have one free weekend. We all looked forward to our chance to travel via train or bus to locations not included on our itinerary. A few of us planned a weekend trip to Marbella; a true gem nestled in Costa del Sol. We bought our own bus tickets, traveled with the locals, and stayed in a little out-of-the way hotel. This, in itself, made for a learning experience. We got to further explore the country, make foreign friends, and truly practice and use our Spanish.

One of my entrepreneurial friends, who studied abroad for an entire semester, knitted scarves and sold them at the local outdoor market. She had fun meeting the people, speaking the language, and making extra money.

Other students enjoyed the cheap rail passes of Europe and traveled on free weekends to surrounding European countries. Of course, the guides and chaperones should always be notified when one is leaving the group. Most importantly, it is safest not to travel alone; try to have others join you.

The six weeks passed so quickly. We traveled to several cities and took in the culture, art, and history. When it was finally time to come home, I truly missed my Spanish family, my university family, and such a beautiful country and experience. I found myself sad to be leaving my piece of Spain behind but appreciated the opportunity to have had such a wonderful experience.

When I returned home, I found that I was ready to see my family and friends, eat a good American hamburger, and reacquaint myself with the comforts of home. My pictures of what I experienced tell good stories and bring great memories. I truly hope to return to those exact spots someday.

Trap Doors

Tips from Mom for Parents

✱ **Discuss safety issues with your traveling student:**
Confronting mishaps and dangers in a foreign country can be much more challenging than dealing with them in the United States. Post 9/11 issues have put more of an emphasis on the importance of knowing and respecting the areas outside of the U.S. and its laws. The sponsor of the program will undoubtedly make available updated information about customs and laws of the particular country. The challenge for parents is to make sure their traveler takes the time to familiarize himself with the information.

✱ **Be aware of differences in communication:** Many cultures have dissimilar ways and habits. Some of our culture's expressions in language can be quite offensive in other parts of the world. As they say, "When in Rome, do as the Romans do!" Respect their ways.

Remember that body language, too, projects a message through hand gestures, facial expressions, and eye contact.

It is important for the student to research the country to which he or she is traveling, in order to avoid unintentional miscommunication.

✳ **Know the acceptable wardrobe:** The way we dress is body language as well. Traveling students should be familiar with the proper dress in the part of the world in which they are traveling. What is accepted here in America might not be appropriate in other countries.

✳ **Apply for—and pack—proper documentation:** Know the types of documentation your student will need such as passport and student visa. Apply well before the journey for either of these! It can take several weeks to receive documents back.

✳ **Design a plan to communicate with each other:** Parents and student should work out a schedule for keeping in touch. Email is the easiest and least expensive form of communication from overseas, with internet cafes widespread in most countries.

Tips from Steff for Students

✳ **If you have the interest and the chance, go!** If you have an opportunity to immerse yourself in another culture by living abroad, you should consider yourself lucky. It can be one of the best experiences in your college career and even in your life. If financing is a challenge, some schools may offer scholarships for students to go abroad. Find out!

First find what programs your college offers. Decide on a country that interests you or is related to your studies. Each program will have an outline of class expectations, schedules and transferable credits. Be aware, however, if you chose to join a group from another university, you may want to see what credits will transfer and count toward graduation. Some credits will not count toward graduation but will certainly count toward living and understanding life!

✳ **Familiarize yourself with your surroundings:** Be sure to explore your new location during daylight so you won't get lost or caught in the dark or in unsafe areas. If you venture out unprepared, you might get stranded with no cabs around and a language barrier. This can be a frightening experience.

✳ **Never carry too much cash:** People from other countries know when there are tourists in town. Assume con artists or thieves might try to take advantage of you. Keep digital cameras, passports, and wallets in a fanny pack or other safe spot.

✳ **Carry a map with you at all times:** Even though it may scream "tourist," always carry a map of the city. If you're not good at reading it, you can ask a local to point to where you are trying to go. In most places, you will find them eager to help you.

✳ **Before you leave, familiarize yourself with the currency of the country:** Spend time learning the currency difference. This will help you when you are spending money abroad. One student from Dickinson College shared her experience of miscalculation when she attempted to use her mother's bankcard in an ATM abroad. She intended to withdraw $20.00 U.S. and withdrew $500.00!

✳ **On your free time, don't travel alone:** Stay in groups. This way, you all can look out for each other.

✳ **Check in now and then with Mom and Dad:** It is good to let your family know your whereabouts. Email is available at schools or internet cafes around the major cities.

✳ **Try to leave your personal problems at home:** Taking personal issues on your abroad experience can ruin the experience for you and others in the group. (There was a girl on our trip who had a serious boyfriend at home, whom she called and cried about everyday. She counted the days until she returned home. I thought she might regret it when she returned, wasting all of her time dwelling on a circumstance far away. Her boyfriend broke up with her the week she returned! She later regretted missing out on much of the experience of living abroad.)

❋ **Make friends abroad and keep in touch!** You will meet tons of people while being away. Not only do you get to know the locals, but also your travel group and other students studying abroad from different schools. I met so many interesting people. Looking back, I wish I had kept in better touch with the friends I made in Spain.

Email:

We received this email from a parent who was very excited to hear from her son studying abroad in Rome. It's communication like this that keeps everyone together.

From: student@email.address
To: parents@email.address

Dear Mom and Dad,
I feel like I'm a little kid again writing you a letter at summer camp. If I remember correctly, I should start the letter off with "I want" or "I need." However, I've grown up quite a bit since those days and I feel I should start this email another way.

Rome is fantastic! I love it. The flight over was good. I sat next to a middle-aged American businessman who was traveling to India. We talked about movies and politics for a lot of the way. By the time I got to Paris, I was a little tired, but I managed to make my way and make my flight. Unfortunately, my luggage did not.

So, Mom, this is when you are probably saying, "I told you so." You were right and I hate to admit it, but I was glad to have the extra pair of boxers and shirt with me.

They still don't have my luggage to me, even with my persistent calling. It is unfortunate because I need to wear pants tomorrow for the Vatican and St. Peter's Church but I'm going to borrow a pair from another kid in my trip. Which brings me to my next topic: the people. They are great. Really interesting people from Virginia, Florida, Ohio, and other places. They are all really nice, and very interested in travel, etc.

So far I have seen the Pantheon, the Forum, the Coliseum, and some other local stuff. On no sleep, I managed to walk around Rome yesterday by myself for a while until I met up with everyone else at the hotel. We move into our apartment tomorrow. The food is amazing and yes, the wine is that much better. As for the running of the bulls trip, I'm in debate at the moment. I'd miss a day excursion to Tuscany which I want to go to. I'm not completely sure, but I'm leaning towards not going at the moment and maybe flying to Florence for the weekend instead. What a life I live!

I'm having a great time, and about to go out to dinner, then out with some other Americans we met tonight, so as they say in Roma—Ciao!

Chapter 11

The Final Phase
Reaching the Golden Door

Reaching the golden door represents a successful end to a journey for both generations: graduation. The journey provides different challenges for different families. Some grads are completely uncertain about what they are trying to accomplish while at college. Other grads will think they know what they want, but lack motivation to try hard. The lucky few will breeze through college and into a job. No matter what the circumstances, open communication and mutual support on the part of both generations can help make this final phase of the off-to-college transition a successful one.

Mom

Now the question I ask myself is, "Where did the college years go?" Four years later, the term "empty nest" has even more meaning. In our family, the transition has been made. No more am I questioning my identity or purpose in the role of mother. Nothing has been lost; new doors have opened in my day-to-day life, and a stronger mother-daughter relationship has been gained. We have survived the transition and now look forward to the next phase.

Proudly observing my child's maturity over these four years has made it easier for me to let go, trust her decisions more, and try to wait for her to ask before I advise.

A Special Bond

Several factors helped Steffany and me through the challenges of this transition. We fulfilled a pledge to each other to maintain open and honest communication. We now know that this was a key factor in maintaining a healthy relationship and understanding each other's needs. By sharing our thoughts and feelings, we have been able to deal with challenges as they have come, one by one. Was it always smooth and easy? No. But we found ways to support one another verbally and nonverbally—with a word, a smile, a hug, or a written reminder. My most difficult challenges were suspending judgments and learning to let go. My determination to trust my daughter played a critical role in this effort.

Having faith and maintaining a positive outlook were other factors that helped make this a successful transition. During our conflicts and disagreements, we made conscious choices not to dwell on past problems or on our fears. Instead, we chose to focus on coping with the particular issue at hand.

Steff

My college experience is still difficult to capture in a few words. "The best years of your life," people say. Well, they have been the best so far, but I don't want to downplay the potential of the rest of my life. I did learn a lot about myself and about life in general. I learned to accept change as an important and inevitable element in personal growth.

At times, I felt somewhat smothered by Mom with her advice and attention to what was going on in my life. I am glad that I learned to communicate openly when I felt she was treating me like a young child. With time, I learned to communicate with less anger and frustration. She developed more trust in me as I took more responsibility. In hindsight, I better understand and have appreciation for her involvement, which I always knew was based on genuine love.

Each phase of my transition had its own joys and challenges. Open communication, a positive outlook, and a good sense of humor helped me to get through. Leaving the nest was not as easy as I initially wanted to believe it would be. I learned, however, that it is what you make of it. And *that* learning has led to my belief that the future will be what I make of it.

The Calm before the Storm

Because of my change in a second major and the intense workload, I graduated a semester late. This upset me because I always saw myself getting my diploma with my closest friends. This wasn't going to be a reality for me. It ended up, however, being a blessing in disguise. I painfully observed many of my friends experiencing panic as they faced graduation and the next step. Too many had no job offers or leads, owed thousands of dollars in student loans, and feared leaving close friends and the world to which that they had grown accustomed. As an outsider looking in, I found this to be eerie. I decided to take the time I had left at school and do what I could to better prepare myself for the future.

The biggest lesson for me was to start the ball rolling with finding a job in my industry. With the job market during the May graduation looking weak, I felt I might have an advantage

> The intangibles of life should never be underestimated. Friendships led me to my first college. Angst drove me to my second. A divine encounter with God moved me to my third. Finally, love persuaded me to stay in one place long enough to graduate.
>
> —Graduate from California

graduating in December. Thanks to my interning and summer jobs, I also had good leads. The summer before my senior year, I worked in a big city, got a taste of its people, layout, and vibe, and decided that that was where I wanted to focus my attention for my future. I began my search for the opportunity and started networking to help fulfill my goal.

More Lessons in Life after College

Suddenly the clarity of it all is apparent and the real real world is staring you in the face. Unless you're going to grad school or moving back in with Mom and Dad, you are facing an empty world and the need to find employment and living space. The institutional safety net is no longer present. You are on your own. Unless you choose grad school, there is no next-step educational system on which you can fall.

Many students today are moving back home with Mom and Dad. This might seem like a cop-out to many, but that is not necessarily true. If you do not have a job waiting for you after graduation, it might be a good idea to go home, get your bearings, go on interviews, make extra cash, and get yourself mentally ready for the next step. Although it might not be your first choice, it may be the best temporary choice. Once again, these details will have to be negotiated with your parents.

I can't urge parents enough, under the right conditions, to let a child move home for at least a bit to allow them to regroup for their move into the next phase. To avoid a permanent situation, set a time limit. Discuss and negotiate house rules. Hopefully, the graduate will get on his feet before too long and live independently.

My advice to students:

✳ Take time and visit the job fairs on campus while you can. Take the word "recruitment" seriously! Ask questions and find what is available and who is hiring.

✳ Intern, intern, and intern! With the extra hours you have free in your junior and senior years, find jobs or internships in your field of interest.

✳ As for your summer jobs, put aside the life-guarding, construction, and waiting-on-tables jobs and get work in the real world of your interests. It not only gives you a feel for whether you like what you have chosen as a career, it helps you to build a resume. Bottom line: You will have experience in your field and have references that count. Many times this can lead to a huge foot in the door and actual employment once graduation takes place.

More to Come

Beware: Once you are in the working world you realize just how good you had it in college! Everything changes: the hours, the dress code, the ability to get an extension on deadlines (try doing that with a status report at your corporate job). And despite all of the grown-up living you are doing, you still feel like a kid inside. Being "grown up" isn't really a feeling you have, it's more of an action you take. There will always be those times of self-doubt and fear of failure throughout life. This isn't something that goes away once you are living in the real world. Just know that with each new experience and challenge, you can learn lessons that will help you through life. Plus, you have your quarterlife crisis to look forward to!

A Special Bond

I can compare my relationship with my mother over these past few years to a game of yo-yo—I have needed her, not needed her; liked her, disliked her; trusted her and questioned her. Although these fluctuations in my moods and attitudes have been stressful on our relationship, they prompted discussion between us and we have steadily built a better understanding of each other. I find it interesting: the older I get, the more I see characteristics of my mother in myself. Sometimes, I laugh about it; at other times, I curse it!

As I look back, despite our differences, I have always felt my mother's love and support. Dealing with our challenges in communication was important for the growth of our relationship during my college years. I know we will continue to face challenges, highs and lows. It's both exciting and scary because you never know what lurks around the next corner. But through it all, I know our relationship will continue to grow.

From Both of Us

This book acknowledges some of the challenges that can exist for parents and children during the off-to-college transition. Nurturing of the parent-child relationship, so critical in a child's early years, is still important as the child enters adulthood. We, as mother and daughter, have shared how we dealt with our own set of challenges. Writing this book encouraged us to look at our relationship without being judgmental. As we go forward to face life's next transitions and challenges, we will strive to remain open-minded and to learn from each other.

In our society, college is a major step in our educational process. All taking that step deserve the best chance to make this a successful transition. Hopefully, for both parent and child, as they close an important door behind them, they clearly and confidently see the next one that has opened ahead.

We received this letter from a student who reflected on the important (and not so important) things he learned in college. Take good advice from him and remember to appreciate all of the people you will meet in college.

To My Friends,

I am a Dynamic Figure. In my days of college, I have learned more outside of the classroom than within, but remain cognitive to the relative importance of both. I've learned skills that have enhanced my well-being and gained knowledge that will last the test of time.

The people that I have met are certainly a prominent and proud element of my four-year career. I have met short happy people, tall angry people, and a bum who could carry a tune. I have met beautiful women with nothing to say, and not-so-beautiful girls that won't shut up. I can tell you to stay away from cheerleaders that work at Hooters, and to stay close to girls that take good notes.

There were many lessons that have been instilled upon me. I have learned to never start a tab, unless of course, the bartender is my friend. I couldn't tell you what time the grocery store opens on Sunday, but I do know when the tavern rings the bell for last call.

Although it has been four long, intense years, it has been one great experience. I will regret nothing, and will remember everything. It is not me that makes me dynamic, but rather the people whom I've met and the good times I've had. For this, I am grateful.

—Graduate, University of Miami

About the Authors

Margo Ewing Bane Woodacre is a graduate of the University of Delaware and has a master's degree in social work from Widener University in Pennsylvania. She has twenty-three years experience in the communication, counseling, and educational fields, and served two terms as a Delaware state senator. Woodacre owns and operates a personnel training and development business, Margo Ewing Bane Services. She lives in Wilmington, Delaware, with her husband.

Steffany Bane is a graduate of University of Miami (Florida) and the recipient of the Outstanding Achievement in Advertising Award. In Miami, she was the online health and beauty writer for *Ocean Drive* magazine. Currently, Bane is a creative copywriter for a major New York City advertising agency. In her free time, she designs T-shirts for her VANEAQUI fashion line.

Together, the mother-daughter team speaks about the emotional and communication challenges of the off-to-college transition to parents, students, and counselors at high schools, colleges, and conferences around the country. Both have made national radio and television appearances.

For more information and to contact the authors, visit frombothsides.com.